The Canterbury Tales

AN ADAPTED CLASSIC

The Canterbury Tales

Geoffrey Chaucer

GLOBE FEARON
Pearson Learning Group

Executive Editor: Barbara Levadi
Adapter: Fiona Simpson
Senior Editor: Bernice Golden
Assistant Editor: Roger Weisman
Art Director: Nancy Sharkey
Cover and Interior Illustrations: Carlotta A. Tormey
Production Editor: Linda Greenberg
Electronic Systems Specialist: José López
Marketing Manager: Sandra Hutchison

ISBN 0-835-90869-0
Printed in the United States of America

10 11 12   06 05 04

Pearson Learning Group

1-800-321-3106
www.pearsonlearning.com

CONTENTS

ABOUT THE AUTHOR

If Shakespeare is the greatest English playwright, then Chaucer can claim the title of the greatest English poet. He is certainly regarded by many as the father of English poetry.

Geoffrey Chaucer was born in England around 1343, the son of a well-to-do wine merchant. He might have spent his entire life in the wine business except for an act of fate. In his early teens, he was sent to serve as a page to Lionel of Antwerp, son of the king, Edward III. For the rest of his life, Chaucer was to be closely associated with the court. He enlisted as a soldier and was captured by the French in 1359. However, he was important enough that someone paid for his release. On his return to England, he served in many royal households. Around 1366, Chaucer married Philippa de Roet. Chaucer and Philippa had at least four children, two sons, Thomas and Lewis, and two daughters, Elizabeth and Agnes. Little is known about three of the children, but the records indicate that Thomas Chaucer had a distinguished career of his own. Like his father, he served as a diplomat and traveled extensively.

In 1367, Chaucer began to serve Edward III. During the next ten years, he traveled around England and overseas on diplomatic missions. At some point, his travels took him to Italy, where he learned about the famous poets Dante, Petrarch, and Boccaccio. Some of their stories were rewritten by Chaucer and included in *The Canterbury Tales*.

In 1374, Chaucer was given an unusual royal gift—the promise of a pitcher of wine every day for the rest of his life. In the same year, Chaucer obtained a rent-free house in London. At this time wool was England's most important export. The king appointed Chaucer the controller of the tax on wool for the port of London. Chaucer was responsible for collecting taxes on the wool. This money helped both to pay the daily costs of government and to finance wars on the continent.

Eventually, Chaucer left London and moved to Kent. From 1385–86, he served as justice of the peace and member of Parliament for the region. But after that, his career and life reached a low point. In 1387, Philippa Chaucer disappears from the records and is assumed to have died. In the same year, Chaucer made the last of his trips overseas. While he still had some duties in Kent, his life seems to have slowed down. It is believed that at this time he began work on *The Canterbury Tales.*

In July of 1389, the new king, Richard II, made Chaucer clerk of the royal works. This meant that he was responsible for construction and repair at ten royal palaces and other properties belonging to the king, including the Tower of London. Later he was appointed keeper of the royal forest at North Petherton in Somerset, another position of great responsibility. Forests included fields, villages and churches, and wooded areas. They were also another source of money for the government. Chaucer was responsible for collecting the fees charged for traveling on forest roads, for grazing cattle, and for collecting acorns to feed pigs.

In 1399, Chaucer returned to London. He died in 1400 and was buried in Westminster Abbey.

CHAUCER'S LITERARY CAREER

Chaucer was a very busy man, but he found time to produce a large amount of work. Unfortunately, many of his works were not preserved, and those that have survived cannot be precisely dated. Probably his first effort was a translation of a thirteenth-century French work, *Roman de la Rose*. Chaucer wrote many poems for the king and his court. *The Canterbury Tales*, however, were written for people like himself, the middle class.

The *Tales* are about everyday life and people. The travelers are a cross section of society from the upper classes to criminals. In his descriptions, Chaucer describes the uneasy balance between what they appear to be and what they are. For example, the Monk ought to be concerned with helping people. However, he doesn't believe in studying or working with his hands. He likes to hunt. Chaucer doesn't tell us if this is good or bad. Instead, he describes the Monk and leaves us to draw our own conclusions. Chaucer's interest in these people and the perceptive but affectionate sketches he draws of them make them stand out in detail. The pilgrims seem alive and almost modern in their weaknesses and interests.

Additionally, *The Canterbury Tales* was written in English rather than in French, which was the language spoken at the court. There were many different versions of English spoken all over England. The dialect Chaucer used, Middle English, was the one spoken in London, and it is the forerunner of the language that we now speak. Chaucer showed that English could be written with a style and power not achieved by earlier authors. That is why Chaucer is regarded as the father of English poetry. It may also be his greatest contribution to literature.

HISTORICAL BACKGROUND

The pilgrimage to the town of Canterbury that Chaucer describes in *The Canterbury Tales* would be a familiar trip to most English people. The shrine of Thomas à Becket was located in Canterbury. Becket, Archbishop of Canterbury, was murdered in 1070 after disagreeing with the king, Henry II. He was later made a saint, and Canterbury became a holy place.

When Chaucer wrote *The Canterbury Tales,* it was customary for people to go on pilgrimages. A pilgrimage was a journey to a shrine or holy place for religious reasons. Pilgrimages were a way of giving thanks for surviving an illness or of seeking a cure for one; of praying for a loved one's safe return from war or of giving thanks for such a return. Pilgrims even went to shrines to ask for success in business. The most important pilgrimage was to Jerusalem, but this trip took many months. Traveling to Canterbury from London took approximately four days.

However, pilgrimages were more than religious journeys. These trips were also a form of vacation, often the only kind available to people. To pass the time while they traveled, pilgrims told stories to keep themselves amused. They also gossiped, argued, and ate and drank to excess. A pilgrimage was often like a carnival in spirit.

Pilgrimages also brought together people from all groups of society. The Knight and the Squire in *The Canterbury Tales,* for example, would be a higher social class than the Miller. There really was a Tabard Inn at Southwark. Its innkeeper was Harry Bailey, who is named in the tales. The other travelers would be familiar figures to Chaucer's audience both from other stories and from everyday life.

CHAUCER'S POETRY

Geoffrey Chaucer wrote in Middle English, which is not that different from the English we speak today. Look at the opening lines from the General Prologue in original verse that appear below.

Whan that Aprille with his showres soote
The droghte of March hath perced to the roote,
And bathed every veine in swich licour,
Of which vertu engendred is the flour;
Whan Zephirus eek with his sweete breeth
Inspired hath in every holt and heeth
The tendre croppes, and the yonge sonne
Hath in the Ram his halve cours yronne,
And smale foweles maken melodye,
That slepen al the night with open yë—
(So priketh hem Nature in hir corages);
Thanne longen folk to goon on pilgrimages,...

We don't know exactly what Middle English sounded like, but we can guess. Here are some hints: the final *e* is always pronounced at the end of the line and within the line; most of the consonants sound the same as they do today and are pronounced in the word. You should also know that each pair of lines rhymes. This is called a couplet and can help you pronounce the words. Now try reading the passage above aloud.

Of the 24 tales Chaucer finished, only two, "The Tale of Melibeus" and "The Parson's Tale," were not written in verse.

THE TALES

The Canterbury Tales was written in the late 1380s and early 1390s. It is a group of short stories told by 30 English pilgrims. The pilgrims are making a 60-mile, four-day trip from London to the shrine of St. Thomas à Becket at Canterbury. The pilgrims are going to tell stories to pass the time on the road. Each one agrees to tell four tales, two tales going and two tales returning. However, Chaucer wrote only 24 stories in all, and four of these were not finished. Chaucer created 29 pilgrims who meet at the Tabard Inn in London and journey to Canterbury together. One of the pilgrims is Chaucer, who is the book's narrator and the "I" voice in the book. Chaucer portrays this man as a simple fellow who takes everything at face value. This lets the poet describe the other pilgrims impersonally while allowing the reader to see their real personalities.

Many of the ideas for the stories in *The Canterbury Tales* came from other writers. For example, the Wife of Bath's tale is based on one of the legends of King Arthur. The Knight's tale and the Cleric of Oxford's tale were both originally from books by Italian poets. Several of the other tales are also based on earlier stories. However, Chaucer rewrote them and made them uniquely his own.

ADAPTER'S NOTE

In preparing this version of *The Canterbury Tales,* we have tried to include as many of Geoffrey Chaucer's tales as possible. While *The Canterbury Tales* was written in verse, we have written an adapted version of a prose translation to make it easier for students to understand. We have changed some of the vocabulary and shortened and simplified many of the sentences and paragraphs. Certain expressions and descriptions have been retained to give the book an authentic Medieval flavor. These phrases have been explained in footnotes.

LIST OF PILGRIMS

Knight . . . . a distinguished soldier
and gentleman

Squire . . . . the Knight's son, also a soldier

Yeoman . . . . the servant of the Knight and
an expert bowsman

Prioress . . . . the mother superior
of a convent

Nun's Priest . . . . her chaplain and secretary

Three Priests . . . . the Prioress's traveling
companions

Monk . . . . a hunting man

Friar . . . . a begging monk

Merchant . . . . a successful businessman

Cleric . . . . a student at Oxford

Man of Law . . . . a successful lawyer

Franklin . . . . a landowner and an epicure

Hat-Maker

Carpenter

Weaver

Dyer

Tapestry-Maker

}

members of
the same guild,
or business
organization

General Prologue

Here begins *The Canterbury Tales*: In April, rain arrives, ending the dryness of March. The new flowers begin to bloom. A gentle wind stirs the young plants in the woods and fields. Birds sing sweetly all day long. When this happens, people want to go on pilgrimages or visit foreign places and faraway shrines. In England, they travel to Canterbury to pray at the shrine there.

I, too, decided to go on a pilgrimage. First, I stopped at the Tabard Inn, where I met a group of twenty-nine people making the same journey. After talking with them, I decided to join their group. Before I tell you about our plans for the journey, let me tell you about my fellow travelers. I shall begin with a Knight.

One of our group was a brave KNIGHT. He loved chivalry,[1] truth, and honor. He had fought in fifteen wars in different countries. Three more times he had fought in single combat to defend our faith. In every battle, he was honored for his bravery. Although he was brave, he was also gentle in his behavior and treated everyone kindly. He had just returned from his travels and, without stopping to change his clothes, went at once on this pilgrimage.

Traveling with the knight was his son, a SQUIRE. He was about twenty years old, and his hair was curly. He had already been in several battles to win a lady's love. White and red flowers covered his clothing, and he rode excellently. He could compose music for songs,

---

1. **chivalry** the noble qualities of a knight, such as courage and honor

1

fight with a sword, dance, draw, and write. He was always kind and helpful, and he waited on his father at meals.

The Knight had brought a servant with him. This YEOMAN was dressed all in green. He carried a bow and arrow, a sword, shield, and dagger.

There was also a Nun, a PRIORESS, whose smile was modest and sweet. She sang very well and spoke French with an English accent. At the table, she never dropped a crumb, nor did she spill sauce on her clothing. In all her actions, she was dignified and imitated court behavior. She kept several small dogs with her, feeding them with table scraps. She was so gentle and softhearted that she would weep if she saw a mouse caught in a trap. Her dress was neat and clean, and on her cloak she wore a pin, an *A* with a crown and the motto *Amor vincit omnia*.[2] Another Nun and three Priests rode with her also.

An outstanding MONK was also traveling with us. He owned many horses, fitted with the finest saddles. He loved hunting and lots of fine food. He did not live by the old rules, preferring to follow more modern ideas. The world would not be helped by his staying in his room and studying, he believed. Nor would it benefit if he worked with his hands. Instead he would ride and hunt the hare. His sleeves were trimmed with gray fur and his hood was fastened with a gold pin. His head was bald and shone like glass, as did his face. He was a fine, fat lord, not pale and ghostly.

There was a FRIAR in the group. He was a well-liked member of his order. He would hear confessions from both the local and the city folk and, for a gift, would forgive them. He knew every tavern in every

---

2. ***Amor vincit omnia*** Love conquers all

town and every innkeeper as well. He preferred their company to that of beggars, and this was only fitting for a man of his dignity. He had his own area to beg, and no one else dared to try his luck there. He could talk a widow into giving him her last penny. If there were arguments on account days, he happily settled them, for a small fee. He didn't look like a poor scholar, but rather like a doctor or a pope.

There was a bearded MERCHANT dressed in clothes of many colors. He spoke very proudly about his own profits and how business ought to be run. In fact, he was so clever that no one knew he owed money everywhere.

A CLERIC from Oxford University[3] was there. He was very thin and his clothing was threadbare. He had promised to enter the church, but had not found a place. But he was not skillful enough to look for a job. When he borrowed money from friends, he spent it all on books. His only concern was studying. He never spoke more than he had to, but when he did, his speech revolved around worthy things.

A MAN OF LAW was also there. He was well thought of—or at least seemed so because his words were so wise. He knew all the cases and decisions from ancient times by heart.

A FRANKLIN rode with the Lawyer. His beard was as white as a daisy, and his face was rosy. He lived for pleasure as a student of Epicurus.[4] He owned a lot of land and always kept the best food in his kitchen and ale in his cellar.

---

3. **Oxford University** a training place for those entering the church
4. **Epicurus** a Greek philosopher whose teachings are often translated as "eat, drink, and be merry"

A HAT-MAKER, a CARPENTER, a WEAVER, a DYER, and a TAPESTRY-MAKER were traveling with us. All wore the uniform of a great and important guild. Their wives thought they should be council-men—they had enough money. After all, it would be nice to be called "Madame" by the neighbors and to go first in church.

These men brought a COOK with them who could prepare delicious meals with very few ingredients. He could roast and boil, fry, make stew, and bake good pies.

There was a SAILOR from Dartmouth I think. He did not worry about honesty. He stole wine from merchants when he transported it from France. When he had the upper hand in battle, he made his prisoners walk the plank. However, he was very good at figuring tides, at using a compass, and steering a ship.

There was a PHYSICIAN trained in astrology. He observed his patients and used the planets and stars to plan their treatment. In fact, he was the perfect doctor, for he could diagnose an illness and immediately suggest a remedy. He had pharmacists who would send him drugs and syrups whenever he asked for them. Each man worked for the other's profit—they were old friends.

There was a good WIFE from Bath, but she was hard of hearing. As a weaver, she outdid all others. She was always first to give money in church. However, if someone cut in front of her, she would lose her temper and give nothing. She had married five husbands and kept other company in her youth, but we won't speak of that now. Three times she went to Jerusalem, and she knew a great deal about traveling. She also knew how to laugh and joke with everyone. She rode well, and wore a fine hat, a riding skirt, red stockings, and spurs on her heels.

There was another man of the church, a poor parish PRIEST. He was truly a good man who gave part of his own salary to those in need. He never abandoned his duties to others, but stayed at home and tried to lead his parishioners by his own example. He not only taught the deeds of Christ and the Apostles, but also followed them himself.

With him, there was a PLOWMAN, his brother, who lived in peace and charity. He would work without fee to help a poor neighbor if he could. He loved his neighbors as himself. He wore a worker's coat and rode a mare.

Finally, there was a Reeve, a Miller, a Summoner, and a Pardoner, a Manciple, and myself.

The MILLER was a big man who always won the prize at wrestling. He could pull any door off its hinges or break it by ramming it with his head. At the top of his nose, he had a wart from which red hair grew in tufts. He knew how to steal grain and charge three times as much for it, but he really was quite honest. He played the bagpipes and led us out of town to music.

There was a friendly MANCIPLE to an Inn of Court, whom other stewards might do well to imitate. This Manciple could buy all the necessary food and drink and still have money left. Isn't it wonderful that an uneducated man could be smarter than a whole group of educated ones? He served more than thirty lawyers who could handle any government emergency, but the Manciple made fools of them all.

The REEVE was a slender, hot-tempered man. He had been in charge of his lord's estate for many years. No one had ever gotten the better of him. He knew all the locals and their minor thefts—and they were scared to death of him. He had secretly stored up great wealth because he knew how to steal indirectly from his lord. The Reeve would loan him money from the lord's own wealth and receive thanks as well as a new coat. He had a good horse and a rusty sword and always rode last in our group.

Next was a SUMMONER,[5] whose face would frighten children. He loved garlic, onions, and strong red wine. When he was drunk, he would only speak in Latin, of which he had learned a phrase or two. That is not unusual: after all, he heard Latin all day, and even a parrot can learn to imitate the Pope. He was a friendly and kind rascal. For the right amount of money, he would excuse a man any deed.

With the Summoner rode a friendly PARDONER,[6] and there was no one else like him. In his bag, he carried pig's bones in a jar. With these relics,[7] he could make more money out of a poor parish priest in one day than the priest earned in two months. But to tell the truth, he could preach very well because he knew that he had to in order to make money.

Now I have told you a little about these pilgrims and why we all met at the inn in Southwark. After a good supper, our Host said, "I know that you are all headed to Canterbury, and I wish you a good trip. However, I have an idea that will make your journey

---

5. **Summoner** an officer of the church court who summoned offenders to appear before the judge. By Chaucer's time, summoners blackmailed suspects by threatening to bring them to trial.

6. **Pardoner** awarded pardons, which were documents approved by the Pope, forgiving people for their sins if they agreed to give money to a charity.

7. **relics** bones that the Pardoner claimed were of saints

much more pleasant. As you travel, each of you will tell two tales on the way to Canterbury and two more on the trip coming home. The one of you who tells the best tales will have a dinner here at the inn paid for by the rest of the company. I will ride with you, at my own expense, to serve as judge. If anyone will not accept my decision, he shall pay for the whole trip for everyone. Now if everyone is agreed, say so at once."

We agreed to his suggestion and to all the rules he had set, and so went off to bed.

The next morning, when dawn began to break, we left the inn. We had not gone far before our Host reminded us of our arrangement and suggested that we draw straws to see who would begin. The short straw fell to the Knight, who said, "Well, since I must start the game, I shall. Now let us ride on, and listen to what I say."

With these words he cheerfully began his tale that is as follows.

The Knight's Tale

Once upon a time, there was a duke named Theseus who was lord and governor of Athens. He was a great warrior. He had conquered the Amazons, and married their queen, Hippolyta. He brought his wife and her sister Emily to Athens to live.

On his way to Athens, the Duke met a group of women crying by the roadside. They told him that the ruler of Thebes would not allow them to bury their dead. Instead, the bodies were left to lie in the fields, where the dogs could eat them. When he heard this story, the duke was so moved that he immediately waged war on Thebes. The Athenians won, and the ruler of Thebes was killed. After the battle, two knights were found on the battlefield. The Duke ordered them taken to Athens and held prisoner there forever. The young men were called Palamon and Arcite.

Year after year, Palamon and Arcite sat in a tower with only each other for company. This might have gone on forever, but everything changed one May morning. On that day, Emily went to walk in the garden. Palamon was pacing his cell. From the window he could see the city and the garden below. He looked down and saw Emily. He fell in love with her immediately. Arcite heard his friend cry out and went to see what was the matter.

"The beautiful woman walking in the garden made me cry out. I do not know if she is a woman or a goddess." Arcite looked at Emily and also fell in love with her.

Palamon was furious when Arcite confessed that he

had also fallen in love with the lady in the garden. He turned on Arcite, saying, "Are you turning against me? You and I promised to help each other no matter the circumstances. I saw her first and loved her first. I wanted your advice, and so I told you. Therefore, you are bound to help me. Otherwise, you are not a true knight."

Arcite replied, "You are the traitor, not me. I loved her before you did. You loved her as a goddess, while I loved her as a woman. Therefore, your feelings are not real.

Anyway, suppose you did love her first. Remember the old saying 'All's fair in love'? Promises are broken for love all the time. However, it is unlikely that either of us will ever win her love. We are both condemned to life imprisonment. Therefore, let us both love her."

They argued for a long time until one day—to cut the matter short—Duke Perotheus came to Athens to visit his friend Theseus. Now, Perotheus had known Arcite in Thebes, and he asked Theseus to release the young man. Theseus agreed with the following conditions: If Arcite was ever caught in any country governed by Theseus, Arcite would lose his head.

When Arcite returned to Thebes, he fell ill with grief because he would never see Emily again. He grew thin and would weep if he heard music. After a year or two of this, Arcite looked at himself in the mirror and realized that he *could* return to Athens. His illness had changed his appearance so much that he could live in Athens quite safely.

One day, Arcite arrived at Theseus's court. He said his name was Philostrate and asked for any kind of job. To make a long story short, he became a servant to the lady Emily. He held this job for a year or two, when he was promoted to serve Theseus himself. There was no one Theseus valued more highly than Philostrate.

Meanwhile, what of Palamon? He sat in prison. But after seven years, he finally managed to escape. He ran away and was forced to hide in a field when dawn broke. Now, it happened that Arcite had chosen this morning to go riding in the same field. Fate[1] brought him to the spot where Palamon was hiding.

Arcite sat down near the hidden Palamon and began to talk about his situation. "I am of royal blood, but I dare not tell anyone my real name. Once I was Arcite, now I am only a servant. How can I hope to marry Emily?"

Palamon heard this speech and was furious. He rushed from the bushes saying, "Arcite, you are a traitor. Either you or I must die. Only I will love Emily. I am Palamon, your mortal enemy."

Arcite drew his sword and said, "I will love Emily in spite of what you say. I will come back tomorrow with weapons for us both. We will fight to decide who shall love Emily." Palamon agreed to this arrangement and the two men parted.

The next day, Arcite returned with the weapons. The two men exchanged no words but immediately began to fight. Palamon fought like a crazed lion, while Arcite was like a cruel tiger. They fought like this for a long time, but Destiny[2] changed the outcome.

That same day, Theseus had decided to go hunting. He rode with Hippolyta and Emily to a grove where he believed there was a buck. Entering the grove, he saw the two men fighting fiercely. Ordering them to stop,

---

1. **Fate** the power supposed to decide events before they happen; the things that will happen to someone
2. **Destiny** like Fate; the things that will happen to someone

the Duke demanded that the two warriors explain the cause of their quarrel.

"Sire," said Palamon hastily, "we both deserve to die. Kill me first, but kill my companion also. He is Arcite whom you banished. He has tricked you for many years by posing as a servant, and he loves Emily. Since we are both to die, I admit that I am Palamon, your enemy, who escaped from prison. I also love Emily and would die in her sight."

The Duke replied quickly, "You have confessed to your crimes, and you will die."

The Queen and Emily began to weep and begged the Duke to show mercy to the two men. Eventually, the Duke was moved by their pleas and began to speak.

"The god of love can make anyone act foolishly. Arcite and Palamon could have returned to Thebes and lived in safety. Instead, they face certain death here because of love. Lovers are fools. Well, I know what it is to be in love, so I will forgive you. However, you must promise never to make war on me but to be my friends." The two men did as he asked. Then the Duke said:

"Now, you both come from good families and are worthy of Emily, but she cannot marry both of you. Therefore, one of you will have to give her up, like it or not. However, I think we will let Fate decide which of you it will be. I have a plan. Each of you will leave and gather one hundred knights. In fifty weeks time, you will return and I will hold a tournament. The one who kills his opponent will marry Emily."

Everyone present thanked the Duke for his wise idea. Then Palamon and Arcite rode home to Thebes.

Theseus began to make arrangements for the tournament. He prepared a huge arena more than a mile round. To the east and west there were white marble gates. Above the eastern gate, there was a shrine to Venus, goddess of love. Above the western gate, there was a similar shrine to Mars, god of war. In the north wall, he built a temple to Diana, goddess of the hunt. Each temple was decorated with paintings and statues. Theseus spared no expense in preparing for the tournament.

Now let us return to Palamon and Arcite. Each returned to Athens with a hundred knights. Every knight who loved chivalry had begged to take part in this tournament. The great King of Thrace rode with Palamon and brought a hundred well-armed men with him. The King of India rode with Arcite and also brought a hundred men. Never before was there such a sight!

The day before the tournament, Palamon rose at dawn and went to the temple of Venus to pray for his success. "If I cannot win Emily," he prayed, "let me die so that I will not care that Arcite weds her." The statue of Venus made a sign that told Palamon his request was granted.

Emily went to the temple of Diana to pray. "My only wish is that you might arrange peace and friendship between Palamon and Arcite. If you cannot do this, grant me only one request. Let the one who wins love me the most." As Emily prayed, a vision of the goddess appeared to her, saying, "Do not worry. The gods have arranged that you shall marry one of them, but I cannot tell you which. Farewell." Emily was amazed, but because she could do no more, she went home.

Later that morning, Arcite walked to the temple of Mars to pray. "Take pity on my pain. I know that I cannot win the tournament without your help. If you help me to win, all the glory will be yours!" As he finished speaking, Arcite heard a voice murmuring, "Victory!" At this sign, he happily returned to his inn.

However, quarreling broke out in the heavens between Venus and Mars because of the promise to Arcite. Finally, Saturn drew up a plan that pleased both sides. "My daughter Venus," he said, "I will make sure that Palamon shall have his lady as you wish. Mars may aid his knight, but I shall help you."

Now I shall stop speaking of Mars and Venus and tell you about the tournament.

The day of the contest arrived, and the arena filled up with people who had come to watch. A herald announced that the Duke had changed his mind. "It would be a foolish waste of blood to fight as if in mortal battle. Therefore, you may fight only with long swords and maces. And if either leader is slain, the tournament will be considered finished."

The battle began and both sides fought fiercely. Eventually, Palamon was captured and led to one side where he could no longer fight. When Theseus saw this, he called out to all the fighters, "Stop! the tournament is over. Arcite of Thebes shall have Emily."

Up in heaven, Venus wept bitterly at the loss of her knight. Saturn said, "Daughter, stop crying. I promised that Mars would have his way; his knight has won the prize, but you shall also be satisfied."

Arcite took off his helmet to let the crowd see his face. Suddenly, there was a terrible noise that caused his horse to rear up in fright. Arcite was thrown to the ground. He was carried to the palace and placed in bed. However, he was in good spirits and kept asking for Emily.

Duke Theseus and his court returned to Athens. Arcite was expected to recover, and no one had been killed. Peace and friendship were restored among all the parties, and a great feast was held.

However, Arcite's injury did not improve. Instead, he grew weaker. The physicians could do nothing for him, and soon it was obvious that he would die. Therefore, he sent for Palamon and Emily and spoke to them like this: "I know that I must die, and therefore I swear that my spirit will serve you. Because of my love for you, Emily, I have fought with my cousin Palamon for too long. I do not know of another man who is as worthy as he or who loves you as well. If you should ever marry, marry him." With these words, he died.

Arcite's tomb was placed in the grove where he and Palamon had fought. All of Athens mourned his death. The funeral ceremony was conducted with great pomp and ceremony. I shall not tell you about the ceremonies or how Emily and Palamon conducted themselves. Let me draw my tale to a close.

After many years, Theseus sent for Palamon and Emily. When the two were seated before him, he spoke thus. "Why do you still mourn for Arcite when he cannot thank you? He died when his honor was at its highest point: what man could wish for more? Therefore, we should leave behind our sorrow and be merry. To that end, Emily, I wish you to take pity on this brave knight who has served you well and to marry him. Palamon, I do not think I will have to persuade you to agree to this."

Thus Palamon and Emily were married. They lived in complete happiness with never a harsh word between them. **Thus ends the Knight's tale.**

The Miller, the Reeve, and the Cook all told tales next. After the Cook had finished, our Host looked at the sun's position in the sky and the length of the shadows and realized that it was ten o'clock.

"Ladies and gentlemen," he said, "the day is one

fourth over. We must waste no more time. Sir Man of Law, tell us a tale now, as you agreed. You gave your consent to be guided by my judgment. Make good your promise."

"Host," the Man of Law replied, "I have no intention of breaking my promise. But I really don't have a tale worth telling, except those old stories that Chaucer has already told. If he didn't use them in one book, he used them in another. He has spoken of almost all the noble wives. So what is left for me to tell?

"In addition, I am not a poet, so my story will be plain in comparison to his. But I don't care. I will speak in prose; let him make the rhymes.

"In fact, I would be without a tale to tell you if it were not for a merchant I knew many years ago. He told me this story, which I will now relate to you."

The Man of Law's Tale

Once upon a time, there lived in Syria a group of wealthy merchants who traveled to Rome to trade. After they had been there for a while, they began to hear stories about the Emperor's daughter, Constance. Everyone spoke of her goodness, beauty, modesty, and kindness. When they returned to Syria, they told the Sultan about this wondrous lady. The Sultan decided that he would marry Constance no matter what anyone said. After a great deal of bargaining, the marriage was arranged, and Constance left for Syria.

There was, however, one problem. The Sultan's mother did not approve of this marriage. She gathered together all of her counselors and spoke to them like this: "My son is about to marry and give up our traditional ways. We have to stop him. If you will all agree to support me, I'll tell you my plan."

All the men swore to die with her if necessary. Then the Sultaness said, "I will pretend to go along with this wedding, but I will have my revenge."

With these words, she dismissed the men and went to see her son. I will not draw out my tale except to say that she told her son that she wished to have a feast to welcome his new bride. The Sultan thanked her on his knees for her kindness. After this, his mother kissed him and went home.

Eventually, Constance arrived in Syria. There were many celebrations across the land. Soon the day came for the Sultaness's banquet.

To make the story brief, the Sultan, his followers, and those who had accompanied Constance were hacked to death by the Sultaness's supporters.

Constance was captured and placed in a rudderless boat. They told her to learn to sail from Syria to Rome. However, they gave her money, food, and clothing.

Constance sailed the Mediterranean for several years until she reached the Straits of Gibraltar. Many times, she thought she would die, but somehow she survived. Finally, she was cast ashore on the English coast near a castle. The warden of this castle came to the shore to view the wreckage and found poor Constance there. She managed to make herself understood to him, but told him that she could not remember her name. The warden and his wife, Dame Hermengild, were so moved by pity for her that they took her in. She, in turn, served them so faithfully that they came to love her.

A knight in the village fell in love with Constance and, when she refused him, plotted her death. One night when the warden was away, the knight crept in and killed Hermengild, leaving the bloody knife at Constance's side. When the warden returned and found his wife dead, he could not believe what he saw. The King of that country, Aella, was asked to decide if Constance was guilty.

All the villagers swore that Constance could not have committed this crime and told the King so. Only the knight said otherwise. The King wasn't sure, so he decided to investigate further. He called together all the people of the village and said that if the knight would swear before them that Constance was guilty, she would be tried.

The knight came forward, but as soon as he spoke he fell down dead at the King's feet. This proved Constance's innocence to everyone. Aella decided to marry Constance.

Who could be sad at this wedding, except for the

King's mother, Donegild? She thought her heart would burst when her son married such a strange woman.

Time passed, and Constance was pregnant. Her husband had to go to Scotland to fight his enemies, so he left his wife with a bishop and the warden to watch over her. In time, she gave birth to a boy who was named Maurice. The warden wrote to King Aella telling him the happy news. The letter was given to a messenger who rode north to deliver it.

This messenger stopped at the court of the King's mother to deliver the news to her also. "Madam," he said, "you will be very happy to hear that the Queen has borne a son. I am going to your son with the news. See? Here is the letter. If you wish to send anything to him, I will carry it for you."

Donegild invited the messenger to stay the night. While he slept, she stole his letter and substituted another. This second letter said that the Queen had given birth to so horrible a creature that no one in the castle was brave enough to stay with it. The King wept when he read this, but he wrote back saying that his wife and child were to be protected until he returned.

Once again, the messenger made the trip and stopped at Donegild's castle. Again, a new letter was placed in his bag. This letter said, "The King commands that the warden shall put Constance and her son into the same ship in which she arrived. This boat will then be set adrift upon the sea. She shall be commanded never to return."

The warden received the letter the next day. He cursed the King for being so cruel but could do nothing. Everyone in the kingdom wept when they heard about the King's order. However, Constance quietly boarded the ship and was pushed out to sea.

Aella returned to his castle and immediately asked

for his wife and child. The warden was frightened but told the King what he had done. You have already heard the story, and I cannot bear to repeat it. The King was shown the letter, and the warden said, "I have done as you ordered." The messenger was taken and tortured until he told them where he had spent each night of his journey. They soon learned that Donegild was behind this wicked plan, and she was killed.

No one can describe the sorrow that Aella felt every day for his wife and son. Therefore, I will turn to events elsewhere.

The Roman emperor learned what had happened to his daughter in Syria and sent an army to punish the wicked Sultaness. The army was victorious and sailed back to Rome. Now Constance had been at sea for five years. Eventually, her ship was overtaken by those of the Roman army, and she and her son were rescued by a senator. He did not know who she was, but took her into his home as a servant. The senator's wife was Constance's aunt, but she did not recognize her niece either. Constance stayed with them for a long time and impressed everyone with her goodness.

I shall now return to King Aella. The King decided to go on a pilgrimage to Rome. As he neared the city, the senator rode out to meet him. The two men entertained each other with great feasts, and it so happened that at one of them, the senator was waited on by Constance's son.

Aella stared at the boy and asked the senator: "Who is that boy?" "I don't know," replied the senator, "He and his mother were found floating at sea. His mother is a good woman, but I do not know who his father might be."

This boy looked like Constance, and this made Aella think that his wife was still alive. But, he thought, how could she have returned to the country that she had left so long ago? That afternoon Aella went to meet this woman. As soon as he saw her, he knew that she was his wife. I will not describe the tears that accompanied their reunion.

Eventually, Aella and Constance returned to England, where they reigned in peace and happiness. However, happiness is often short lived. Aella died a year later. Constance returned to Rome and lived with her father until death separated them. **Here ends the Man of Law's tale.**

The Shipman, the Prioress, and I were next to tell our tales. When I had finished, the Host turned to the Monk and said, "Cheer up, Sir Monk. You must tell a tale now. Don't spoil our fun; go ahead."

"I'll do my best to tell you a tale or two," the Monk replied. "I'll tell you some of the stories which I have learned. These tales are about men who were once powerful. However, even the powerful often fall into misery."

(The Monk proceeds to describe the downfall of many famous men. I shall relate only two.)

The Monk's Tale

The Monk begins the tale of Hercules: There once was a man named Hercules who slew many monsters and performed many deeds. He is still famous in song and story. We all know his twelve mighty labors.

He slew the lion of Nemea, which no weapon could kill, by choking it. Then he killed the nine-headed Hydra. This monster had one head that was immortal. If one of the other eight was chopped off, two more would grow back. Hercules used a burning stick to burn the neck as he cut each head off. Then he buried the immortal one under a rock. Next, he had to clean the Augean stables. Augeas had thousands of cattle and their stalls had not been cleaned for years. Hercules changed the direction of two rivers and made them flow through the stables. Why, he even had to agree to carry the heavens on his shoulders so he could get the golden apples! After many other labors, he descended into the underworld. There, he stole the three-headed dog Cerberus and brought him above ground.

But even Hercules eventually met his death. His wife made him a shirt and dipped it in Centaur's blood. When Hercules wore the shirt, it burned his skin. When he tried to pull it off, it pulled the flesh from his bones, but he wouldn't die. Finally, Hercules killed himself.

Thus fell the mighty Hercules! Let all men beware how Fortune[1] plots to overthrow them.

The Monk's tale of Count Ugolino of Pisa: A short distance outside of Pisa stands a tower in which Count Ugolino and his children met their fate.

The Bishop of Pisa had accused the Count of treason. So the Count and his three children were locked away. They were given very little food and water. What they were given was barely enough for all of them. One day, the jailer did not deliver their food at all. Ugolino heard the jailers shut the tower gates, but said nothing to his children. Yet, he was afraid that his enemies meant to starve him to death.

After several days, the youngest child died in his father's arms. When the father saw his dead son, he began to bite his arms in grief. His children thought he bit his arms from hunger and cried, "Father, don't do that! Eat our flesh so that you can live." Within a day or two, these children also died. Ugolino himself finally died of grief. Thus a mighty man reached the height of power and then was betrayed. Fortune took his greatness from him, and he met his end in jail. **Thus ends the Monk's tale.**

"Stop," said the Knight. "You have made us all sad. I think it would be good to hear a tale about a poor man who rises to fortune. We have heard enough tales about how the mighty are fallen."

---

1. Fortune the power thought to bring good or bad luck to people

"Well spoken," said our Host. "You have told enough of tragedy, Sir Monk; tell us a merry tale now. Tell us something about hunting."

"No," said the Monk. "I have no wish to tell a foolish tale. Let someone else speak now."

Then our Host spoke to the Nun's Priest, saying, "Come, sir, tell us something to cheer us up."

The Nun's Priest's Tale

Here begins the Nun's Priest's tale of Chanticleer: Once upon a time, there lived a poor widow. She didn't have much money; she didn't have many animals. But she managed to support herself and her two daughters. She had three pigs, three cows, and a sheep named Mollie. In a yard enclosed by sticks and a dry ditch, she kept a rooster named Chanticleer. He was the most famous crower in the whole country. His crowing marked the time more accurately than any clock, even the one in the church. As soon as the sun rose, he crowed perfectly. He was also very handsome. His comb was redder than coral; his bill was black and shiny; his legs and toes were blue; his nails were whiter than lilies; and his feathers were the color of bright gold.

This rooster ruled over seven hens, but his favorite was called Lady Pertelote. Polite, gracious, friendly, and well behaved, she'd held Chanticleer's heart since she was seven days old. As the sun rose, it was a joy to hear them sing together. For in those days, or so I've been told, animals and birds could speak and sing.

Early one morning, Chanticleer sat on his perch. Next to him sat Pertelote. Chanticleer began to groan like a man having nightmares. "Whatever is wrong?" she asked.

"Don't be upset," he answered. "I just had a terrible dream. I dreamed that I was in such danger that I'm deathly afraid. I dreamed I was walking up and down in our yard when I saw a beast like a dog. He was red, and his tail and his ears were black. He had a small nose and two bright eyes. I almost died just looking at him. No doubt that is why I cried out."

"You are a coward," said Pertelote. "I don't love you anymore. I can't love a coward. Can you really be afraid of dreams? Dreams come from eating too much. Now, when we fly down from this roost, I will find some herbs that will help you. Don't be afraid of a silly dream."

"Madam," he replied, "many people have had dreams that foretold the future. I read in a book about two men who went on a pilgrimage. They could not find a place to stay in town, and so they separated. One of them had to sleep in a barn, while his friend found a room at an inn.

"Before dawn, this man dreamed that his friend came to see him and cried, 'I will be murdered tonight! Help me or I will die!' The man woke up, but then went back to sleep. He thought his dream was only foolishness. He dreamed the same thing twice. He had a third dream later that night. This time, he dreamed that his friend appeared before him and said, 'I'm dead now. I was murdered for my money. Get up early in the morning, and go to the west gate. There you will see a cart. My body is hidden in it.'

"The next day, as soon as it was light, the man went to look for his friend. When he arrived at the barn, he was told that his friend had left. The man remembered his dream and ran to the west gate. There he saw a cart heading out of town. 'Stop that cart,' he shouted. 'My friend's body is hidden in it!'

"The townspeople rushed to the gate and over-turned the cart. In the middle of it, they found the murdered man's body. Murder will out; we see that all the time. Murder is so terrible that it cannot be hidden forever. From this, you can see that people should be afraid of dreams.

"I read in the same book about two men who were going to sail over the sea to a distant land. The night before their trip, one of the two dreamed that a man stood by his bed and said, 'If you sail tomorrow, you will be drowned.'

"The man woke and told his friend what he had dreamed. His friend laughed. 'No dream,' he said, 'will make me change my plans. Dreams are nonsense.' So he went, leaving his friend behind. Before the voyage was half over, the ship sank, and all the men aboard were drowned. So you see, dreams can foretell the future.

"I know from my dream that I will have trouble. But let's change the subject. When I see your sweet face, I can ignore dreams."

Chanticleer flew out into the yard and strutted around proudly. He wasn't afraid anymore. But suddenly, a terrible thing happened.

A tricky red-and-black fox had lived near the yard for three years. The night before, he broke through the hedge into the yard. He lay quietly in a patch of weeds until the middle of the morning, waiting for his chance to kill Chanticleer. Meanwhile, Pertelote and the other hens bathed happily in the sunshine. Chanticleer sang cheerfully and watched the butterflies. Then suddenly, he noticed the fox lying in among the weeds. "Cock-a-doodle-doo," he cried out, though his heart was beating fast with fear.

"Where are you going?" asked the fox. "Are you afraid of *me*? I only came to hear you sing. You have an angel's voice. I have entertained both your mother and father in my house. I would like to entertain you also. When men speak of singing, I can truthfully say that I have never heard anyone sing like your father. He would close his eyes, stand on tiptoe, and sing for all he was worth. Now sing, sir. Let's see if you can imitate your father."

Chanticleer was so flattered that he never suspected the fox's evil plans. He stood up high on his toes, closed his eyes, and began to crow. The fox leaped up, seized Chanticleer, and began to carry him toward the wood. The hens began to cry; nothing could compare with the noise they made.

The widow and her daughters heard the hens shrieking. They rushed outdoors in time to see the fox carrying the rooster away.

"Help! A fox!" they cried. The neighbors ran after him with sticks. The dogs ran after him. The cow and her calf ran after him. Even the pigs ran after him. The villagers brought trumpets and blew them to try and frighten the fox.

In spite of his fear, Chanticleer spoke to the fox. "Sir, if I were you, I'd tell them to go back. You are almost at the wood now; they'll never catch you. Tell them that you plan to keep this rooster and eat him, too!"

The fox answered, "I shall." But the moment he opened his mouth, Chanticleer broke free and flew high into a tree.

"Oh, Chanticleer!" cried the fox. "I've frightened you, haven't I? I didn't mean to. If you'll come down, I'll tell you what I really want. I'll tell you the truth, honestly!"

"No," said Chanticleer. "I was a fool to believe you the first time. I won't be fooled a second time."

"No," said the fox. "I am the fool. I had you firmly in my grasp, but I let you go. I should have kept my mouth shut."

That's what happens when you are careless and believe in flattery. Those of you who think this tale is foolish because it is about a fox and a rooster, make sure you understand the moral: Pride goes before the fall.

Thus ends the Nun's Priest's tale.

The Wife of Bath's Tale

"My life gives me the right to speak of the troubles that often occur in marriage. Since I was twelve years old, I have had five husbands. Now some people will say that you should marry only once, but God never mentioned any number, so why should people consider five marriages a sin?

"I beg you all, if I speak my mind, don't be offended. I mean only to amuse you. So, as I said, I'm an expert on trouble in marriage. I've been the cause of some of it myself. Three of my husbands were good and two were bad, but I treated all of them the same. Three of them were rich and gave me all their land and money. Once they did this, I no longer made any effort to respect them. They loved me so much that I didn't value their love. A woman will try everything to win love when she doesn't have it. But I had them completely in my power, so why should I trouble to please them? I used to scold them so terribly that they were delighted when I spoke kindly to them.

"But my fourth husband was a bad man. I ate my heart out because he loved another woman. But I got my own back. Because I was attractive to other men, he would become very angry, and I tormented him with jealousy. He died when I came back from Jerusalem. His tomb isn't very much to look at. It would have been a waste of money to bury him grandly.

"Now I'll tell you about my fifth husband. He was so mean to me that I'll feel the pain until my dying day. But I believe that I loved him best because he was so stingy with his love. We women always want the thing we cannot have easily. Forbid something to us, and that's what we want. Give us a thing, and we will run away.

"I married my fifth husband, Jenkin, for love, not money. He'd been a student at Oxford. He was staying with a friend of mine whom I often visited to hear the gossip. Once, Jenkin, my friend, and I went walking in the fields. My husband was in London at the time. The scholar and I enjoyed each other's company so much that I told him that if I were a widow, he could marry me. I always planned ahead to my next wedding. A mouse isn't worth a jot if he only has one hole to run to. If that hole falls in, he's done for. So I always like to prepare the way, just in case.

"When my fourth husband was laid out, I wept as a good wife should. But since I had already prepared for the future, I didn't really shed many tears.

"My husband was carried to the church, and Jenkin was one of the crowd of mourners. When I saw him, I gave him all my heart. To be truthful though, he was only twenty years old, and I was forty. But I was still lively, good-looking, and rich. I never cared what a man looked like so long as he pleased me.

"Well, to make a long story short, Jenkin married me at the end of the month. I gave him all my lands and money, and was I sorry! He wouldn't let me have anything. Once, he struck me so hard on the ear because I tore a page from his book that I became deaf. He forbade me to do this and forbade me to do that, but I wouldn't listen to him. I hate a person who tells me all my mistakes.

"Let me now tell you why I tore a page out of his book. He had a book that he read night and day. Whenever he had a moment's rest, he'd read this book about wicked wives. There were wives from the Greek myths and wives from the Bible and even more wives.

Every time a man feels that a woman has rejected him, he sits down and writes that women can't be trusted.

"When I saw that he would read that book all night, I tore three pages out while he was reading and hit him with my fist. He fell down backward and then jumped up and hit me on the head. I collapsed and lay as if dead. When he saw how still I was, he was frightened, but finally I came round. Eventually, we made up. He gave me the rule of the house and his money. I made him burn his book. After I had gained complete control, we never had another argument. I was as good to him as any wife from Denmark to India, and so was he to me. Now, if you'll listen, I'll tell you a story.

The Wife of Bath's tale: Many hundreds of years ago, when Arthur was king, all England was filled with spirits. Nowadays, no one can see these spirits because the countryside is full of homes, churches, villages, and towns.

Now, Arthur had in his court a young knight who was out riding one day when he saw a maiden walking by the river. In spite of her struggles, he forced himself upon her. This caused a great deal of anger at the court, and the knight was condemned to death. However, the Queen and her ladies begged the King for mercy. So the knight was turned over to the Queen, who would decide his fate.

One day, the Queen said to the knight, "You are not sure yet if you will live or die. I'll save you if you can answer one question. If you can't give me the right answer, you shall die, but if you give the correct one, you may live. I don't expect you to be able to tell me right now, so I will give you one year to learn the correct response. Do you agree to this?"

The knight agreed to the Queen's demands. What else could he do? So the Queen set his test. He had one year to learn what women want most. When he heard this question, the knight sighed with sorrow. How could he ever learn the answer? Finally, he decided to go wandering and return at the end of the year with whatever answer he could find. He said good-bye and set out on his journey.

He asked the question every place he could, but nowhere could he find two people who agreed. Some said that women like money best. Some said honor, some said clothes, some said widowhood and remarriage. Some said that our hearts are best pleased when we are flattered and fussed over. I'll tell you the truth: that's close to the right answer.

Some said we love to be left free to do as we want without complaint, or that we love to be thought wise and sensible, that we want to be considered trustworthy. But that's not true. We women can't keep a secret.

The knight grew more and more distressed when he realized he couldn't learn what women love best. But the day had arrived on which he had to return. As he rode and worried about his fate, he passed by the edge of a forest. There he saw more than two dozen women dancing. He approached them hoping to learn something. But when he got close, the women vanished into thin air. The only person left was an ugly old woman, the ugliest you can imagine.

The old woman stood up and said, "Sir Knight, no road passes through this wood. Tell me what you are looking for. Maybe I can help you. Old people are very wise."

"Good woman," said the knight, "I am condemned to die unless I can find what it is women want most. If you can tell me, I'll make it worth your time."

"Give me your hand," she said. "Promise me that you will do the first thing I ask you to do, no matter what it is, and I'll tell you what you want to know."

The knight quickly agreed. "Then," said the old woman, "I can promise you that you are safe. The highest woman in the land won't dare to deny what I'll tell you. Now enough talking." Then she whispered something in the knight's ear and told him to be happy.

The old woman accompanied the knight on his return. When they came to the court, the knight said he had returned as promised. He said he was ready to answer the Queen's question. Many noble ladies, many maidens, many wise widows assembled to hear him, and the Queen herself sat in judgment. The knight was ordered to appear. The crowd was commanded to keep silent so that he could tell his listeners what thing women love best.

The knight didn't stand there stupidly, but, in a voice just loud enough for all the court to hear, began to speak. "Your majesty," he said, "in general, women want to rule over their husbands and their lovers, to be the power behind them. Though you may decide to kill me, this is what women want most. I'm here as you commanded."

In all the court, there wasn't a wife, maid, or widow who disagreed with him. They all agreed he deserved to live.

When she heard this, the old woman jumped up. "My queen," she said, "I taught this knight the answer to your question. In return he agreed to do the first thing I asked of him. Before the court, Sir Knight, I ask you to honor your promise and take me as your wife. You know I saved your life. If I speak untruthfully, say so now."

"I know what I promised," cried the knight. "But please ask for something else. Take all my money, but let me go free."

"Though I am ugly, old, and poor," she said, "I don't want all the gold in or above the earth. I want to be your wife."

"No!" cried the knight. "It would dishonor my family." But in the end, there was nothing he could do. Everyone agreed that he must keep his promise to the old woman and marry her.

Some people will want to hear about the celebrations that followed the wedding. What the people wore, what they ate, and how they danced and made merry. But I will respond briefly—there were no celebrations. No one feasted the bridal couple. There was no dancing. The knight wed the old woman in the morning, and for the rest of the day he hid. Like an owl who dislikes sunlight, the knight flew away because he was so unhappy at having such an ugly wife.

That night, his new wife faced him. "Husband," she said, "do all the men at King Arthur's court behave like this? I'm the one who saved your life. I never hurt you. Why are you behaving so badly? What did I do? Tell me, and I will fix it."

"How can you?" the knight asked. "What ails me cannot be repaired. You are ugly, you are old, and you are of low birth. Is it any wonder that I regret my promise? I wish I had never met you!"

"Is this why you are so unhappy?"

"Yes."

"Now, sir," she said, "if I want to, I can change all this in no time. But you must treat me properly. You spoke about my low birth. The kind of position you mean comes from having money. That doesn't matter at all. The most important thing is doing good deeds. If a man helps his neighbor, what does money matter? We may claim to be noble because we have inherited money and titles, but we must inherit goodness also. Noble is as noble does. Therefore, although my ancestors were humble, I hope that I live in charity and grace.

"You scold me for being poor. A poor man need not fear thieves. A poor man knows himself. In addition, he is not taken in by those who only value him for his money or position. Poverty makes for hard work. It also adds wisdom. I think poverty is a pair of spectacles that lets a man see his true friends.

"Next, you scold me for being old. Even if the books don't say so, it is generally believed that you should treat an old man with respect. You even call him 'Father' to be polite. Because I'm old and ugly, you don't have to worry that I'll run off. I will be a faithful wife to you. Nevertheless, you do not want me as I am.

"Therefore, choose now," she said. "I will give you two choices. One, I can stay as I am, old and ugly, but a true and humble wife to you. Two, I can be young and beautiful, but then you must take your chances that I might meet someone else. Choose for yourself, whichever you want."

The knight thought and thought and finally replied, "My dear wife, I leave the choice to you. Make the decision that pleases you the most. I don't care what it is. I will be ruled by you."

"Then have I gained control of you?" she asked. "I can choose and rule as I please?"

"Yes, I think it would be best."

"We are no longer enemies then," she said. "I promise that I will be both to you. I will be both beautiful and true. If I break my promise, you may do whatever you want with my life. Turn around and see if I am not as I promised."

The knight did as she asked and saw that she was as young and beautiful as she had said. The knight was true to his word and allowed his wife to guide him in all that he did. She, too, kept her promise and was faithful to him throughout their lives. And so they lived in perfect happiness until their deaths.

May we all have young, loving husbands and the luck to outlive them." **And thus ends the Wife of Bath's tale.**

Now, while the Wife had been speaking, the Friar had been casting unpleasant glances at the Summoner. Finally, he said to the Wife of Bath, "Madam, may you have a long and happy life! You have said many true things, but there is no cause for us to speak of anything but happy matters as we travel. Let's leave preaching to the clergy. If it shall please this company, I will tell you a funny story about a Summoner. You all know from his very title that nothing good can be said about such a man. I hope that no one will be upset by my story."

At this, the Host then spoke, "Now, sir, you should be kind and polite. It is only fitting for a man in your position to behave in a proper manner. We don't want any arguments among ourselves. Tell your tale, but leave the Summoner alone."

"That's all right," said the Summoner. "He may say what he likes. When my turn comes, I'll repay him in his own manner. I shall tell him what an honor it is to be a licensed beggar. I'll also tell about all manner of crimes of which friars are guilty. But I won't go into that now. No, let him speak. I'll bide my time until it is my turn."

"Peace, gentlemen, enough of this!" cried our Host. Then he turned to the Friar and said, "Tell your tale, sir."

The Friar's Tale

Once upon a time there lived in my part of the country an archdeacon.[1] Now, this was a man of great importance. He would swiftly prosecute people for witchcraft, slander, robbing churches, and breaking wills and contracts. If a priest told him that someone hadn't paid his church taxes, he would fine them severely. If the offering was too small, he would punish them also. Now, the archdeacon had a summoner who helped him with his work. There wasn't a better man at his job in all of England. This summoner kept a group of spies who reported everything to him. They told him what every man and woman in the area was up to. The summoner then used the information for his own profit.

In fact, this summoner knew more about bribery than I could possibly tell. He made great profits for himself that his master knew nothing about. He would call a man before him and threaten to excommunicate[2] him. This man would then gladly give the summoner money for his purse and buy him dinners at the local tavern. Since the summoner made his living this way, he devoted all of his time to it, and it was very profitable.

One day, this summoner rode to summon an old widow to court. He wished to rob her, so he pretended that he had a case against her. As he rode along, he

---

1. **archdeacon** a church official ranking just below a bishop
2. **excommunicate** a way to punish for sins—People could be excluded from the church for disobeying religious law. At the time, that was a very serious matter.

happened upon a yeoman riding ahead of him. The yeoman carried a bow with sharp arrows and wore a green coat and a black-fringed hat.

"Sir," said the summoner, "welcome."

"Welcome to you, good fellow. Where are you riding? Do you travel far?"

"No, I am going to collect some rent which is owed to my lord."

"Are you a bailiff?[3] For I am one also," responded the yeoman. "I am new to this area and would like to know you. If you ever visit my district, I will entertain you properly."

Now, this summoner was ashamed to admit that he was merely a summoner because the position was so hated. Instead, he quickly fell in with the other's suggestion, and the two swore eternal brotherhood. Thus, they rode on together talking happily.

"Where is your home?" asked the summoner.

"Far to the north. I hope some time to see you there. Before we separate, I will give you directions to my home so you will not miss it."

"As we ride along, will you teach me how I can most profit in my job?" asked the summoner. "Don't hold anything back, but tell me how you do business."

"To be honest," replied the yeoman, "my income is very small. My lord is a stern master, and my job requires a great deal of work.

Thus, I make my living by extortion. Everything I spend, I get by force. I can speak no plainer."

"Don't be ashamed," said the summoner. "I do the same thing. The only things I won't take are those that are too heavy to carry. My conscience doesn't bother

---

3. bailiff an administrative official who collected taxes and served as a judge for a district

me. I couldn't live any other way. But, sir, tell me your name, for I can see that we are much alike."

The yeoman began to smile and replied, "I am a demon. My home is in hell, and I ride the earth looking for victims. The things I find are my income. We are indeed alike. You don't care how you get your riches, and neither do I."

"I thought you were a yeoman," said the summoner. "You look like a man, just like me. Do you have a specific form in hell when you are there?"

"Of course not. We have no form there, but we can assume any form we like. We assume whatever form enables us most easily to take in our victims," explained the demon.

"Why do you go to all this trouble?" asked the summoner.

"Oh, for many reasons," answered the demon. "But the day is almost half over, and I have gotten nothing yet. I shall attend to my duties rather than debate with you. In any case, you aren't smart enough to understand these things. But you asked why we work so hard: because it is our job. Sometimes, we torment only the body. Sometimes, we torment body and soul. And at other times, we torment only the soul. If a man can resist us, he is saved. If he cannot, he is ours.

"As to our bodies, sometimes we rise in the bodies of the dead. Sometimes we adopt a form that will please those we seek. But don't worry about that now. Soon enough, you will know everything you could wish about these matters. From your own experience, you will be an expert. But let us ride. I wish to keep company with you until you leave me."

"No," said the summoner, "I won't do that. We swore brotherhood, and I would keep my promise. Let us proceed with our stealing. You take whatever you want, and I'll take what I want. That way we can both live. Let us share equally and be as brothers."

With these words, they rode on.

Near the entrance of the town, they saw a cart stuck in deep mud. The cart driver beat the horses and shouted at them, but they could not move the cart. "The fiend take you both! I have had enough of you. Let him take everything, horses, cart, and hay!" he cried.

The summoner drew alongside his companion and whispered in his ear, "Go on then. Take it all. He has given it to you."

"No, that is not what he meant," the devil replied. "Ask him if you do not believe me. Or wait and see what happens next."

At that moment, the horses began to pull the cart slowly from the mud. "Bless you both!" cried the driver. "Now my cart is out of the mud. What a fine pair of horses you are."

"See," said the demon, "what did I tell you? He said one thing, but he thought another. I get nothing here."

The two passed through the town, and when they had traveled a little farther, the summoner began to speak. "There is an old woman living here. She won't give away a penny, but I mean to have twelve pence from her no matter what. If she won't give me the money, I will summon her to court even though I know of no crime she has committed. Since you seem to be unable to make your expenses, watch me and learn how it is done!"

With these words, the summoner knocked at the widow's door.

"Who is there?" asked the woman. "Good day, sir. What do you want?"

"I have here an order for you to appear before the court. If you don't, you will be excommunicated."

"But I cannot. I have been ill. I cannot ride or walk that far without dying. Could I have a copy of the charges, Sir Summoner, and answer them through my agent?"

"Pay me, oh, twelve pence right now, and I will clear you of all charges. My master will get all the money, not I. Come along; I haven't all day. Give me the twelve pence."

"Twelve pence!" the woman cried. "I don't have such a sum. I am old and poor. Show me some charity, I beg of you."

"No," replied the summoner. "May the foul fiend take me if I let you off."

"But I am not guilty!"

"Pay me," he said. "I will also take away your cooking pot for the fine you owe me from the last time you were summoned before the court. You did not pay then either, and I paid the fine for you."

"I was never called before the court in all my life. You are a liar! Go to the devil yourself, and take my pot with you!"

When the demon heard her curse, he spoke to the woman, "Now, dear mother, is what you are saying the truth? Do you really want this?"

"If he won't tell the truth, let the devil take him," she repeated.

"No, old witch," said the summoner, "I have no intention of changing my story. I only wish I could take everything you own."

"Now," replied the demon, "don't be upset, but you and this pot are mine. You shall go to hell with me and learn everything that you wish."

The fiend then grabbed the summoner and took him away to that place where summoners are usually found.

"Ladies and gentlemen," said the Friar, "always remember that temptation waits to make prisoners of us all. Keep your faith, and you will withstand the fiend. And pray that these summoners repent of their own evil deeds before the fiend seizes them!" **Thus ends the Friar's tale.**

The Summoner was so angry at the Friar's tale that he positively shook.

"Ladies and gentlemen," he cried, "I ask only one thing. Since you have listened to the lies of this Friar, now let me tell a tale. It does not surprise me that this Friar claims to know a great deal about demons. It is well known that friars associate with devils. But enough of this. I will tell a tale now that shall repay this Friar.

The Summoner's Tale

In a district in Yorkshire, a friar used to go about preaching and begging. One day, this friar had preached in a certain church. He asked the people to give money for masses to be said for the souls of the dead. Next, he asked them to contribute money so that religious houses could be built. However, he urged people not to give money to places where there was waste and reckless spending. Instead, he told them to give money to places where holy works were always practiced.

When the people in church had given him whatever money they could, he left. He would not stay once their wallets were empty. Instead, he went from house to house begging meat and cheese or grain. Another friar traveled with him, carrying a pair of ivory tablets and a pen. When anyone gave them food or money, they would write the giver's name down in their books. The friars always promised to pray for everyone whose name was written down.

A servant traveled with them. He carried a sack on his back. In this sack, he would put whatever the friars were given. As soon as the friar left a house, he erased the names which had been written down. Instead of praying for these people, he mocked them and told them lies.

"No, you lie!" said the Friar.

"Be quiet," said our Host. "Get on with your tale, Sir Summoner, and don't leave anything out."

"Indeed I won't," said the Summoner, "I'll tell the whole story!"

So the friar went from house to house until he arrived at one home where he was always well fed. The man who owned the house was sick and lay in bed.

"Good day to you, Thomas!" cried the friar. "I have eaten many a good meal here!" So saying, he sat down comfortably on a bench. His companion and servant had walked on to another town where he planned to spend the night.

"Good friar," said the sick man, "how have you been? I haven't seen you in several weeks."

"I have been working very hard," said the friar, "I have said many prayers for you. Today, I was preaching at the church in the village. I think I did my best. But I will tell you about it. I spoke of the need to be generous and spend money wisely. And I saw your wife there. Where is she?"

"She will join us soon," said the man.

At this moment, Thomas's wife entered the room. The friar greeted her with a warm kiss.

"I hope that you won't mind if I speak to your husband for a little while," said the friar. "I don't believe that these local priests are good at getting men to confess. I give my best effort to preaching and studying. My only purpose is to spread the holy word."

"I wish you luck with him!" said Thomas's wife "Scold him well! Although he has everything he could possibly want, he is always angry. I can do nothing to make him happy."

"Oh, Thomas," cried the friar, "this is terrible. Anger is a sin. I will speak to you about that."

"Now," said the wife, "before I leave you, what would you like for dinner? I shall make you a meal."

"Madam," said the friar, " I don't want much. A few slices of chicken, some bread, and after that the head of a pig. But, please, don't go to any trouble for me. Those few things will be plenty."

"One last thing before I go," said the woman. "My child died two weeks ago, shortly after you left."

"I know already!" said the friar, "I saw it in a vision. I saw him carried up to heaven! Two of my fellow friars saw the same thing. All the members of my community rose and sang holy thanks for this vision. Believe me, sir and madam, when I say that our prayers are better than those of ordinary men. We live a simple life. We don't eat or drink a lot as do other men. To pray well, you must fast and live a holy life. Food and clothing are enough for us, even if they aren't very good.

"We begging friars are sworn to a life of poverty, charity, and holiness. Therefore, as you can see, our prayers are more acceptable than yours.

"But listen, Thomas, everywhere you look, you will see that our profession is honored. Just like a hawk rises into the air, so our prayers rise up to heaven. Thomas, if you were not our friend, you would not be successful. My fellows and I pray every day and night that you will regain your health and strength."

"I don't feel any better in spite of all your prayers!" Thomas said, "Over the years, I have given a lot of money to all sorts of friars. But I haven't gotten any better. I have almost used up all my money!"

"Oh, Thomas, why do you give money to many different friars?" asked the friar. "Isn't it enough if I, or rather my group, pray for you? You are ill because you haven't given us enough! When you divide something, it is never as strong as when it is whole. I don't want any of your money for myself. I do, however, want your money for my religious house. We have always helped you with our prayers. Now you must help us to build a new church.

"Listen, Thomas, you lie here full of anger and argue with your wife. What good does that do? You shouldn't make trouble! Anger is a form of pride. Both anger and pride are sins. I could tell you many stories about the damage caused by these sins. It is very dangerous to give an angry man a lot of power. I will give you an example.

"Once upon a time, two knights rode out together. Now it so happened that only one of them came home. He was immediately accused of murdering his companion. The judge said, 'You have killed your companion, and for this act, I condemn you to death.' A third knight was ordered to take this man out and execute him. They had ridden only a little way when they met the man everyone thought was dead. The three men immediately returned to the judge. They said, 'The knight did not kill his companion. Here he is, alive.' 'You should be dead,' said the judge. 'now the first knight must die because I already condemned him. The second knight must die because I thought he was already dead. Because I thought he was dead, I condemned his companion to die. And the third knight must die because he has not done what I ordered.' Then he had all three men executed.

"Therefore, Thomas, give up your anger and pride.

They will only lead you to trouble. If you will confess your sins to me, I will forgive you."

"I will not," cried Thomas. "I have already confessed my sins. I don't need to confess again to you."

"Then give me some of your money to help us build our church," said the friar. "We have eaten many poor meals to save money. Yet, we have hardly finished laying the foundation. We owe forty pounds for stone alone! Now, Thomas, help us as we have helped you!"

Thomas nearly went crazy with anger. "I have given you enough money!" he cried. "I cannot give you what I don't have. I have told you already that I have given away all my money."

"If you do not give us money," said the friar, "we will be forced to sell our books. How can we continue to teach if we have no books? Now, Thomas, help us!" And with these words, the friar got down on his knees.

"I will give you one last gift for your house," said Thomas. "But you must promise me that you will share it equally with all the other friars."

"I swear it," said the friar. "See, here is my hand. I will do as you ask."

"Now, look in the bed behind my back to find what I have hidden there." Thomas said, "When you have found it, you can share it with your brothers."

The friar searched but found nothing in the bed until Thomas suddenly broke wind.

The friar jumped up in anger. "You did that on purpose! You will regret this insult!" he cried.

He left the sick man's house and found his traveling

companion. The two men then went to the lord of the town. When they arrived at the lord's manor, the friar was shaking with anger. He complained that he had been gravely insulted and asked that Thomas be punished. After the friar had told him the entire story, the lord said, "Let the man be! He is obviously mad. Eat your dinner, and don't worry about him."

Now, the lord's squire had heard every word of all the things which I have told you. He spoke up saying that Thomas's gift could be equally divided between the friar and his brothers. "All that is needed," he said, "is a day with no wind, a wagon wheel with twelve spokes, and the friar and twelve others from his order. Each of the twelve would then kneel at one of the spokes. This friar would kneel at one side of the axle. Thomas would be at the other and repeat his act. Thus, each man would share in the gift!"

Everyone, except the friar, agreed that this was the only solution. In this way, the friar could share his "wealth" with his brothers as they all deserved. **Thus ends the Summoner's tale.**

When the Summoner had finished, the Host turned to the Cleric and said, "Sir, you sit there so quietly. I think you must be thinking about some philosophy, but there is time enough for that later. Now you must tell us a tale. Make it a merry one. Don't preach like a monk; save your lofty words and images for your writing. Speak simply so that we can understand you."

"Host," said the Cleric, "I shall try to do as you ask and as we all agreed. I shall tell you a tale I learned from a cleric many years ago. His name was Francis Petrarch,[1] and he was a fine poet. Before he wrote the text of this poem, he composed a prologue in which he described Italy. He spoke of the lands of Lombardy and Piedmont, of the Apennine mountains, and of the Po River and its source—but this would take much too long for me to tell, so let me begin my story."

---

1. **Petrarch** Italian poet and scholar who lived 1304–1374

The Cleric of Oxford's Tale

On the western side of Italy, at the base of a mountain, there is a fine country called Saluzzo. It was ruled at one time by a lord named Walter. He was a very handsome young man and strong and honorable also. He never worried about the future, but only of immediate pleasures like hunting. He let the management of his land rest in the hands of others. Worst of all, he would not marry. This fact so upset his people that one day they went to see him and spoke like this:

"Lord, while you and everything you do have always pleased us, we do have one request. It would make our happiness complete if you would marry. None of us is getting any younger, lord. All men must die sooner or later, and we cannot predict when this will happen. If you should die without an heir, what would happen to us? Therefore, we ask you to agree to marry. If you will do so, we promise to find you a wife from the greatest family in the land. Then it will seem an honor, not a duty, to marry."

"My people," replied Walter, "you are asking me to do something I never thought about. I will agree to marry if it will make you happy. However, let me choose my own wife. Children do not always take after their parents. The noblest parents cannot always produce a noble child. Therefore, let me marry where my heart tells me to. I ask only one more thing from you. Whomever I decide to marry, you must promise to honor her as if she were the daughter of an emperor. If you will not agree to this, let us speak no more about the matter."

The people happily agreed to all of Walter's requests, asking only that he set a day for the wedding. This was done, and the people returned home.

Not far from the palace where Walter lived, there was a small village. Here, the poor people of the area lived. Among these people was an old man named Janicula. He might have been the poorest of all of them, but for one thing. He had a daughter. Her name was Griselda. Griselda was pretty, but her true beauty lay in her actions. All day, she worked in the fields tending their sheep. At night, she would slice and boil roots and herbs for their supper. She had a hard life, but she never complained.

Walter had seen this young woman often when he passed through the village. He thought about Griselda's behavior and decided that she was the one he would marry.

The day set for the wedding drew near, but no one knew who the bride was to be. Many people wondered about this and in private asked, "Has he decided to break his promise? Will he never marry?"

Meanwhile, Walter had jewels and clothing prepared for Griselda. The plans for the feast went ahead, and the palace was decorated. But still Walter would say nothing. Finally, the morning of the wedding arrived, and Walter set out with all his nobles. They rode to the village where Griselda lived with her father, and Walter called to them. Griselda immediately fell to her knees before him and listened quietly to what he had to say.

"I wish to marry your daughter," said Walter to Janicula. "I know that you are my loyal subject. Will you therefore agree to take me for your son-in-law?" Janicula could do nothing but agree.

Walter then turned to Griselda and spoke thus: "You know that it is your father's and my wish that you marry me. Do you agree to this? Or would you like to think about it some more? In addition, will you agree to be ruled by me? If you will agree to this, I will announce our engagement right now."

Griselda answered, "Lord, I am unworthy of this honor, but I will agree to what you have asked. I will never willingly disobey you in act or thought."

Walter took her by the hand and led her out to meet his people. "This is the woman I will marry, and I ask you all to honor her." The ladies of the court dressed Griselda in her new clothes and jewels, and then the Marquis married her. She was placed on a white horse and rode back to the palace.

To cut the story short, Griselda quickly became beloved of the people. No one could remember that she was the daughter of Janicula, even people who had known her from birth. She had always been kind and gracious. Every day, these virtues seemed to increase. Her reputation for goodness spread around the world. Griselda could manage a household and, when Walter was away, the kingdom. She possessed such wisdom and judgment that people thought she had been sent by heaven to solve injustice.

In time, Griselda gave birth to a baby girl. Everyone was happy that a child had been born and felt sure that a son would follow.

Now as it often happens, Walter began to think that he needed to test his wife and prove her loyalty. Time passed, but he could not get the idea out of his head. Personally, I think it is cruel to treat a wife in this way and cause her unnecessary pain and fear.

One day, Walter went to his wife and said, "Griselda, you know that I found you in poverty and raised you up to this high state. Now, not all of my nobles are pleased with this. In fact, since the birth of our daughter, they have begun to complain more loudly. Now I want to live peacefully with them as I have always done. Therefore, there is only one solution, and it concerns your daughter. This is not what I want to do, but what my people wish me to do. I cannot do this without your consent. Remember the promise you made that day in the village when I first asked you to marry me. Show me the patience that you promised."

Griselda listened to her husband's speech without saying a word. Finally, she said, "My lord, my child and I are completely in your care. Do as you like. There is nothing which pleases you that can displease me."

Walter was pleased with her reply but pretended not to be. He left the room and sent a servant to Griselda. "My lady," said the man, "I have come for the child."

He said no more, but grabbed the baby. Griselda could do nothing. Finally, she asked to be allowed to kiss the child good-bye and then let the man go. She never spoke of the matter or suggested by a look or a glance that she held her husband to blame. Instead, she went on as though nothing had happened.

Four years passed and Griselda gave birth to a son. When two years had gone by, Walter again felt the need to test his wife.

"Wife," said Walter, "you already know that my people are unhappy about our marriage. Since the birth of our son, it has grown worse. The people say that when I am dead, the blood of Janicula will rule. I must pay attention to this unrest. Therefore, I have decided to deal with this boy as I did with his sister. I am warning you now so that you can control your sorrow."

"I have always said that I will obey your every wish," she replied. "If you order that my son be put to death as my daughter was, so be it."

The same man arrived and took the boy from his mother. Walter was amazed at Griselda's patience. He knew that, next to himself, she loved her children best in the world.

Now I ask you women, was this not enough? What more could a husband do to test his wife's faithfulness? But there are people who cannot give up an idea once they have gotten hold of it. Walter was just such a man. He was determined to continue testing his wife.

While nothing in Griselda's attitude changed, the people began to whisper against Walter. They believed that the children had been murdered. To be called a murderer is a terrible thing, but Walter was determined, and nothing would move him. He decided to test his wife again. He told Griselda that the Pope had ordered him to leave her and to marry again. This would settle the trouble between his people and himself. Griselda was very upset when she heard this, but she would do whatever her husband ordered.

Walter told Griselda that she would have to leave the palace. She could take with her anything she had brought to the palace. Griselda told him that because she had brought nothing, she would take nothing. So he took away all of her fine clothes and jewels and sent her back to her father. Griselda left the palace without a word and returned to her humble life.

The people followed her weeping and cursing Walter but could do nothing. Griselda, however, never spoke a word against Walter or by any sign showed anything but that she loved him. Her father soon heard what had happened and ran from his house. He found his daughter in the street, followed by the weeping crowd. Covering her as best he could with her old coat, he led her back into their humble home.

Thus, this jewel among wives lived for a time with her father. Never once did she suggest that her husband had done anything but treat her correctly. She cared for her father as she used to do and never regretted the past or looked back to it with longing.

Sometime later, Walter called Griselda to the palace and said to her, "I don't have enough servants to prepare the palace for my wedding. You know the way I like things, so I would like you to take care of the arrangements." Griselda agreed.

Walter's brother-in-law arrived. He brought with him Griselda's two children, whom he had been caring for all these years. Everyone thought that the girl was the bride-to-be and wanted to see her. They all marveled at her youth and beauty. Many said that Walter was right to marry such a noble girl. The serious-minded people in the town condemned the crowds for valuing appearance over virtue.

Griselda also went to see the girl. Walter saw her standing there and asked her what she thought of his new bride. "I never saw anyone lovelier," replied Griselda. "I ask only one thing of you: do not torment this young girl. She has been gently brought up, and I do not think she could endure it as a woman brought up in poverty could."

When Walter saw that Griselda was still as patient and happy as ever, he began to pity her.

"This is enough, Griselda," said Walter. "I have

tested your faith in every possible way, and now I know your virtue. You are my wife. This girl is our daughter, and this boy our son and my heir. I had them taken from you so that I might test you. I did not do these things from cruelty, but to test your love for me."

When Griselda heard this, she fainted from happiness. And when she recovered, there was much weeping as everyone praised her. Walter strove so hard to please her that it was a joy to see their happiness. Griselda was dressed in beautiful clothes and jewels, and the family was reunited once more.

Thus ends the story of patient Griselda. She and Walter lived out their lives in happiness and peace. Their daughter was married to one of the finest lords in Italy. Griselda's father was brought to the palace to live out his days. The son succeeded his father and married happily, but he did not test his wife. **With this, the Cleric ended his tale of patient Griselda.**

"Now ladies and gentlemen," said the Cleric, "remember that no one expects wives to imitate the absolute virtue of Griselda. But everyone should be as loyal in times of trouble as he or she can be.

"Let me say one more thing, and then I'll stop. Today, I don't think you could find more than a single Griselda in an entire town. And so, because of the affection that I have for the Wife of Bath, let me sing a song that I think you will like. Enough of seriousness, listen to my song:

"Griselda and her patience both lie buried in Italy. Therefore, let no man try his wife's good nature hoping to find another Griselda, for he will fail.

"Oh, wives of great wisdom, never keep quiet. Don't ever let a cleric write a story like this about you. Be like Echo; always answer back. Don't be fooled; take control.

"You wives who are strong as oxen, stand up for your rights. Don't let men do you wrong. You weak wives should be like tigers in battle, and always speak your mind. Don't fear or respect men. Bind them to you with jealousy. Let them stay home and weep and worry while you go out and have some fun!"

The Merchant told his tale next. When he had finished, the Squire began to tell us a tale. Before he could finish, the Franklin interrupted. "My goodness," he said, "I admire your wit. Why as you get older, no one will be able to match you! I wish my son was as clever as you. Alas! He likes to gamble, but he always loses! He'd rather spend time with servants than with a person such as yourself. If only he would learn some good manners!"

"Enough about manners!" cried our Host. "You know, Sir, that each man must tell a tale or two or lose the bet. Therefore, get on with your tale."

"I wouldn't intentionally break my word," the Franklin replied. "I only hope my tale will please you."

The Franklin's Tale

Once there was a knight called Arveragus who loved a lady, Dorigen. After many years of faithful service, she agreed to marry him and to be his true wife until she died. In turn, the knight swore to obey her always and to follow her advice in all matters, as a lover should.

After they had been married for a year, Arveragus decided to go to England to seek honor in battle. Dorigen wept and sighed and took no interest whatsoever in life. She would go for long walks along the cliffs watching the ships sailing to shore. But this only made her sadder. "Among so many ships," she said, "isn't there one that will bring my husband home?" At other times, she would sit on the edge of the cliff, thinking. But when she looked down at the rocks below, she grew afraid again. What if her husband's ship crashed?

Seeing that walks by the sea only upset Dorigen more, her friends tried to amuse her with dancing, games, and picnics in the garden. Among the dancers was a young squire named Aurelius who had been in love with Dorigen for the last two years. He had never spoken of his feelings for her but swore that he would die if he did not.

One day, Dorigen fell into conversation with this young man. Seeing his chance, Aurelius said, "Madam, I know that my love for you is wrong and can only lead to a broken heart, but I do love you. Have mercy on me or I will die."

"I had no idea you felt this way," said Dorigen. "Aurelius, I will never be untrue to my husband in word or deed. That is my final answer. But since I see you are so unhappy, I will promise you one thing. I will be your love when you remove all the rocks that prevent ships from landing safely on the coast. If you do this so that not a pebble remains, then I will love you best among men."

The miserable Aurelius went home and prayed to Apollo for a flood that would cover all the rocks, but nothing happened. Finally, his brother told him about a magic book he had seen once when he was a student. This book showed how a magician could make a castle appear out of thin air. Perhaps a magician could make it seem as if the black rocks on the coast had disappeared. Then Aurelius could claim his love.

To make a long story short, the two brothers set off for the city to find a magician. When they neared the town, they met a young scholar walking on the road. He greeted them and said, "I know why you are here." Aurelius accompanied the scholar, who was magician, to his home. After supper, the two men discussed the magician's fee for removing all the rocks on the coast. The magician said he couldn't do it for less than a thousand pounds, and even then it was a bargain.

Aurelius said, "What is a thousand pounds? If I ruled the world, I would give it all to you. I shall pay you what you ask."

The next morning, Aurelius and the magician traveled home. Finally, the great day arrived and the magician cast his spell. For a week or two, it looked as if all the rocks had disappeared. When he saw this, Aurelius went to see his beloved. "Lady," he said, "the last thing I want to do is cause you pain. But I must remind you of the promise you made to me. You swore that if I could make the rocks on the coast disappear, you would be my love. I have done as you ordered. Go and look. You will see that I have kept my side of our bargain. Now I ask that you keep yours."

Dorigen stood like a statue after Aurelius left. "What am I to do?" she asked. "I never thought he would perform such a task." She went home and wept, but would tell no one what had happened. Arveragus was out of town, and there was no one to console her. "I can only escape through death or dishonor. I must choose one or the other. I would rather die than know that I had been false to my husband." For two days, she lamented and planned to die.

On the third day, Arveragus returned home and asked why she was weeping. At his kind words, Dorigen began to weep even more. "Curse the day I was born," she said and told him everything that I have told you. I won't repeat it all now.

"Wife, I would rather die for your love than see you fail to keep your promise. A promise must be kept." But as he spoke, he burst into tears. "I ask only one thing—tell no one what has happened. I'll bear my sorrow. I won't give anything away, so no one will judge you."

Arveragus then called a squire and maidservant, telling them, "Take Dorigen wherever she asks."

Aurelius met Dorigen in the middle of town and asked her where she was going. "To keep my promise," she replied, "as my husband ordered."

Aurelius thought for a moment. He felt sorry for her and for Arveragus who loved her, but would not let her break a vow. He decided that it was better for everyone if he released her. Briefly he said, "Madam, tell your husband this: I see his great love for you, and I know your pain. He would rather be dishonored than have you break your promise to me. I would rather suffer than come between you. Therefore, I release you from your promise and will never mention it again. Now, farewell to the best wife I ever knew."

Dorigen fell to her knees and thanked him and then rushed home to tell her husband what you have just heard. Arveragus and Dorigen lived happily together for the rest of their lives.

Aurelius, however, still had to pay the magician a thousand pounds. "What shall I do? I'll have to sell my property and become a beggar. I can't stay here. Perhaps I can pay the magician over time."

He took five hundred pounds from his strongbox, brought it to the magician, and asked for time to pay him the rest. "I'll repay my debt to you even if it means I must become a beggar. Please give me two or three years to pay off the rest."

"Didn't I keep my end of the bargain?" asked the magician. "Didn't you get the woman you wanted?"

"Yes, you kept your bargain, but no, I did not win my lady," said Aurelius and proceeded to tell the magician everything that had occurred. "I felt so sorry for Dorigen that I released her from her promise and sent her back to her husband. There is nothing more to say."

"You have all behaved so kindly toward one another. If a scholar cannot behave as well as a knight and a squire, then I shall indeed be ashamed. I release you from your debt as if we had never met. I won't take a penny from you. You fed and housed me. That is enough. Farewell." The scholar then mounted his horse and left.

"Ladies and gentlemen, the Franklin said, I have one question for you: Who do you think was the most generous? Tell me before we journey another mile. I don't know any more. My story is finished." **Thus ends the Franklin's tale.**

Next, the Physician told a sad story. When he was done, the Host said, "You've made me so unhappy that I must hear a merry tale next, or my heart will surely break! My fine friend, yes, you, Sir Pardoner, tell us a happy story or some jokes now." However, the rest of the company cried that the Pardoner would tell some obscene tale and demanded that he tell something moral.

"Indeed I shall," said the Pardoner, "but first I must think of one."

The Pardoner's Tale

"Ladies and gentlemen, when I preach in a church, my message is always the same—*Radix malorum est cupiditas*—'Greed is the root of all evil.'

"To start, I announce where I come from, and then I show my documents. First, I show my license from the cardinal so that no one will interrupt me when I speak. After that, I tell my tales. Then I show documents from popes, cardinals, bishops, and patriarchs, and I speak a little Latin to stir the congregation up. Then I bring out my glass cases and show my wares. I have a shoulder bone from a sheep set in metal. 'Good friends,' I say, 'if this bone is dipped into a well, and you have a sick cow or sheep, simply wash the animal's tongue with some of the well water. It will instantly be cured. If the farmer who owns the well takes a drink every day for a week, his livestock and goods will multiply. And this water cures jealousy; let a wife make soup with this water, and her husband will trust her always.' Then I show them a mitten, and I tell them that the wearer of this mitten will see his grain multiply.

"Next I tell them, 'If there is any man or woman in this church who has committed a horrible sin and is ashamed to ask forgiveness for it, that person will not be able to make an offering to my relics. But anyone who is free from such a burden can come up and make an offering. I will pardon him by the authority granted me by the Pope.'

"In this way, I have made over a hundred pounds a year ever since I became a pardoner. I only preach about greed and similar sins. This makes the people more generous when I ask for contributions. My only purpose is profit! I don't care a wit about their souls! Many sermons have grown out of evil purposes. Sometimes, I will preach to flatter someone and thus gain some new honor for myself. At other times, I quarrel with someone and get my revenge with a sermon. Even if I don't name the fellow in question, everyone knows whom I mean. He cannot escape being wrongly slandered. This way I spit out my hatred under the guise of holiness.

"I preach for nothing but greed; therefore, I always preach about greed. Thus, I preach about the sin that I practice. While my sermons don't make me repent, I can turn others away from it and make them repent. However, as I have said, my main purpose is my own gain, not their souls. But that is enough about this.

"Now I use many old tales in my sermons. The people like them because they are easy to remember and repeat. I will now tell you a tale that I use often. I may be a dishonest man, but I can tell a moral tale. Because that is what you want to hear, be quiet and listen to what I say."

Here begins the Pardoner's tale: Once upon a time in Flanders, there lived a group of three young men. They spent all of their time gambling, eating, drinking, and swearing. Believe me when I say that all sin springs from greed. If you do not believe me, look at the Bible or read the philosophers. Greed weakens the mind and allows sin more freedom. Gambling is the mother of lies and deceit and manslaughter, as well as being a waste of time and money. As for swearing, I pray you give up your oaths both large and small, for swearing leads to anger and anger leads to murder. Therefore give up your oaths. But now on with my tale.

Early one morning, the three men sat in a tavern. They heard a bell ringing, which signaled that a corpse was being carried to its grave. One of the three called to a young boy, "Go and find out whose corpse that is."

"Sir," said the boy, "I know who it is. He was an old friend of yours. Last night, he was sitting on a bench, drunk as can be, when he was killed. Death, that stealthy thief, had stolen his life away. He comes for all the people in this country. During this plague, he has killed thousands, and you never know when he will come. My mother taught me to be ready to meet him at any time."

"It's true," said the innkeeper. "This year in a near-by village, Death has killed men, women, children, and servants. I think he lives there. I would be careful in case he takes it into his head to hurt you."

"Is he so dangerous?" cried the drunk. "I'll go and look for him. Listen, friends, we three have always been united as one. Let's swear brotherhood and slay this thief Death. Anyone who kills so many deserves to die himself."

The three of them promised to live and die for one another. They swore fierce oaths that Death would be dead, if they could find him. Then they rushed out of the inn and started toward the village that the innkeeper had told them about.

They had traveled about half a mile when they met a poor old man. He greeted them politely, but they laughed at him. One of the youths asked him, "Why are you all wrapped up so that only your face is visible? Why did you live to be so old?"

The old man stared him in the eyes and said, "Because, although I walked all the way to India, I couldn't find a man who would trade his youth for my old age. So I must remain old. Even Death won't take my life. So I walk around and knock on the earth with my stick, saying, 'Dear mother, let me in. Look at me. When shall I rest?' But she will not let me in, and therefore, I am pale and wrinkled.

"But, sirs, it is rude of you to speak like this to an old man. I have neither done nor said anything wrong. You should treat me with respect. I will give you some advice: treat an old man as you would wish to be treated when you yourself are old. Now I take my leave of you. May your journey be pleasant and short."

"Oh, no, you don't, old man," cried the second youth. "Just now you spoke of Death who is killing all our friends. I think you are his spy; so tell us where he is or you shall regret it. I believe you are part of his plot to kill all young people!"

"Sirs," the old man replied, "if you are so eager to find Death, turn down this path. I left him under a tree in that wood. He won't hide from your bragging. Do you see that oak tree? You will find him waiting for you there!"

The three youths ran to the oak tree, and under it they found what seemed to be almost eight baskets of gold coins. They forgot to look for Death after that. They all were so happy at the sight of the shining coins that they fell to the ground. Finally, the worst of them spoke to his companions.

"Brothers," he said, "hear me out. I am not a fool even if I do make jokes. Fortune has given us this money so that we can live the rest of our lives in ease. Who would have guessed that we would have such luck today? If we could carry this money home, then we could celebrate. However, we cannot transport it during daylight. If we do, people will accuse us of being thieves and hang us. Therefore, we must carry it at night. Let us draw straws. The one who draws the shortest will go to the village and fetch bread and wine for us. The other two will guard the treasure until

he returns. Then tonight, we will transport it some-where safe."

He held the straws out and each man took one. It happened that the youngest of the three had to fetch the food, and he set out immediately. He had not been gone long, when the first began to speak, "You see that our companion is gone, but the gold is still here. What if I could arrange things so that instead of splitting the gold three ways, we only had to divide it by two? Wouldn't I have done you a favor?"

The second answered, "How can you do that? He knows that we stayed here with the gold. What can we do? What can we say to him?"

"Will you keep the secret if I tell you?" asked the first.

"I swear," replied the other.

"In that case," said the first, "we are two, and the two of us are stronger than one. When he returns, you pick a fight with him. As you scuffle, I will run him through with my sword. Then when he is dead, we will divide this gold between the two of us." Thus these two agreed to murder the third as you have heard me describe.

Now the youngest had gone to town to buy the food, and as he walked, he kept thinking about the coins. "If only it were possible for me to have all this gold! Then no one could live as well as I would!"

It occurred to this scoundrel that if he killed his two companions, he could indeed live as he wished. So he found an apothecary[1] and persuaded the man to sell him some strong poison to kill rats.

---

1. **apothecary** a pharmacist

The apothecary said, "I will give you such a strong poison that no creature in all the world could eat or drink of it and not die immediately."

The youth then ran to another shop where he purchased three large bottles. He put the poison in two and kept the third clean for himself. Then he filled the bottles with wine and returned to his companions.

I won't make a long story out of this. The two killed the third as soon as he returned, just as they had plotted. When that was done, one said, "Now let's sit and drink. Later, we will bury his body." However, he picked up one of the poisoned bottles and after drinking from it passed it to his friend who also drank deeply. They both died immediately. That was the end of these two murderers and of the poisoner. **Thus ends the Pardoner's tale.**

"Now, gentlemen," continued the Pardoner, "my holy pardon can cure you all from sin so long as you offer silver pennies, or silver brooches, spoons, or rings. Ladies, give me some of your best wool, and I will forgive all your sins as though you had just been born. That is how I preach. I will not deceive you.

"Oh, but I forgot one part of my story. I have relics and pardons in my bag that are the finest in the land. The Pope himself gave them to me. If you give me money, I can give you a new pardon every mile of the journey. You're lucky to have me on this trip. If an accident should happen, if someone should fall from his horse and break his neck, I can absolve him of sin before his soul leaves his body.

"I suggest that our Host be first, after all he is the biggest sinner. Come here and make the first offering. You can kiss every relic for a penny. Open your purse now!"

"I won't," cried the Host. "You'd swear your old pants were a saint's relic if you thought you could make a profit!"

The Pardoner was so angry that he couldn't say another word.

Before this could go further, the Knight interrupted. "No more of this! Sir Pardoner and you, Sir Host, shake hands. Let's laugh and enjoy ourselves as we did before." And so we rode on.

The Canon's Yeoman's Tale

We had ridden only another five miles when two men overtook us. One man was dressed all in black and rode an aged horse which was flecked with sweat. His yeoman's horse was sweating so hard, it could barely walk.

I began to wonder what kind of men they were, until I noticed the way the first man wore his cap. When I saw how it was attached to his cloak, I decided that he was a canon.[1]

When this canon had caught up with our party, he began to shout: "I have ridden fast because of you. I wished to travel with your merry group."

His yeoman was also very polite and said, "Sirs, I saw you ride from the inn and told my master. He is so eager to accompany you and join in your fun."

"Your master is most welcome," said our Host. "Can he tell any kind of merry tale with which to entertain us?"

"My master knows more than enough of fun to please you all. But he is more than good company. It would be to your great advantage to get to know him better."

"Isn't he a cleric?" asked the Host. "If not, then what is he?"

"No, sir. My master is much more than a cleric. Why, I bet if he wanted to, he could turn this road on which we travel upside down and pave it all with silver and gold."

"If what you say is true," said our Host, "then tell

---

1. **canon** a member of the church who serves in a cathedral

me why your master pays so little attention to his own appearance. His coat is dirty and ragged. Why doesn't he buy better clothes if he can do all that you claim?"

"Why?" exclaimed the yeoman. "He shall never prosper! It is a fault in his character. In that respect, I consider him foolish. He has a great intelligence, but he misuses his abilities."

"Tell us about your master. Where do you live?"

"We live in the outskirts of a town. We hide in corners and blind alleys where robbers gather."

"And you, sir," inquired the Host, "why is your appearance so odd?"

"I am used to blowing on the fire that we use in our work. I do not waste time in studying my face in mirrors. Instead, I study the science of changing metals. In spite of all our efforts, however, we always fail. We fool many people by making them think that we can make two pounds for every one. Yet, it is a lie. We always hope to succeed, but it has not happened yet."

While the Yeoman was talking, the canon heard every word. He turned on the man saying, "Be quiet! You are telling things that should be kept secret."

However, the yeoman would not be silenced, and when the canon saw this, he ran away.

"Now we'll have some fun!" declared the Yeoman. "I won't have anything more to do with him. I am now so deep in debt that I will never get out. Still, I will get my revenge on that man by telling you all his secrets! Before I have finished, you will see that no matter how honest a man seems, he can be a thief! Let me tell you a tale to prove what I say."

Here begins the Canon's Yeoman's tale: In London, there lived a priest who was so nice and helpful that even his landlady wouldn't take a penny from him. He had plenty of money and always dressed well. But that doesn't matter. I will tell you how this canon brought this priest low.

One day, the canon came to this priest and begged for the loan of some gold, which he promised to pay back in three days' time. The priest gave him the money, and the canon left. Three days later, he returned the money to the priest, which made him very happy. The priest commented that he didn't mind loaning money to someone who was so trustworthy.

"What! Did you think I couldn't be trusted!" exclaimed the canon. "I have never failed to repay a loan. And since you have been so good to me, I shall show you some of my secrets and teach them to you also."

The priest quickly agreed. The canon asked for some mercury and some coals so he could begin his work. Next, he took a crucible[2] from his pocket and showed it to the priest.

"Now, put an ounce of the mercury in the crucible, and I will turn it into silver right before your eyes. I have a very expensive powder that will do this."

Everything that the canon ordered was done. The priest set the container on the fire, and the canon threw a powder into the crucible to fool the priest. I don't know what it was made of, but it wasn't worth a penny. Next, the canon told the priest to put the coals over the crucible. While the priest was busy arranging the coals, the canon placed a fake coal containing an ounce of silver on the fire. When the fake coal had been burned, the silver filings inside it fell down into

---

2. **crucible** a fire-resistant container used in the heating of metals

the crucible. The priest, of course, knew nothing about this. He thought the mercury had turned to silver.

The canon then shaped a mold out of chalk and threw it into a pan of water. "Put your hand in the water," he commanded the priest. "You will find silver if you search for it." What the priest didn't know was that the canon had secretly slipped silver into the pan.

"I shall make one more test," said the canon. "Then some day when you need silver, you can try this."

The priest was busy preparing the fire as he had been told to do. Meanwhile, the canon held in his hand a hollow stick in the end of which he had put an ounce of silver filings sealed with wax. Once again, he threw the powder on the flames, and then he stirred the coals with his stick. Well, needless to say, the wax melted and the silver filings fell into the crucible.

The priest was so happy at the results that he offered the canon all his possessions in return for the formula.

"Well," said the canon, "it is very expensive. There is only one other man in England who can do this. If it were not for the friendship that you showed me earlier, you would certainly pay more."

The priest fetched forty pounds and gave it all to the canon in return for the formula.

"Sir," said the canon, "I don't want praise. Don't give away my secret. For if men knew what I could do, they would surely kill me."

"Why, I would rather lose everything than betray you," said the priest.

"You have proven yourself a true friend," said the canon. "Thank you and good-bye!"

The priest never saw him again. The day finally came when the priest wanted to test out his formula. But, of course, it didn't work. See how he was tricked, and that is how the canon fools everyone. **Thus ends the Canon's Yeoman's tale.**

Our Host turned to the Cook and said, "Wake up, you! What's wrong with you, sleeping all morning? Are you drunk?" Before the Cook could reply, however, his horse threw him and he lay on the ground unable to pick himself up. It took great pushing and pulling to get him back in the saddle. And then the Host spoke to the Manciple:

"I believe this man would tell a stupid story because he is so drunk. Tell your tale. Don't worry about him."

"Very well, sir," said the Manciple. "Listen to what I have to say."

The Manciple's Tale

Here begins the Manciple's tale of the crow:
The old books tell us that Apollo used to live on earth.
We all know that he was a great musician and archer.
But did you know he kept a crow in his house that he
taught to speak? This crow was white as snow, and he
could imitate the speech of anyone. In addition, he
sang more sweetly than the nightingale.

Apollo also had a wife in his house. He loved her
more than life itself and did everything he could to
make her happy. However, the truth is that he was
jealous and wanted to keep her locked away.

Now, everyone knows that if you place a bird in a
cage, it will long to be free. It doesn't matter if you
give it the best food and drink or if you take care of it
most lovingly; it will long for freedom. Even if its cage
is of the best gold, this bird would rather live in a
desert. And so it will try to escape if it can. This bird
will always want freedom.

The same is true of a wife if she is not given her
freedom. She will want to escape from her cage, no
matter how beautiful. And so it was with Apollo's wife.
Although he was a handsome man and faithful, he was
jealous and guarded her closely.

In spite of everything, Apollo was deceived. His wife
loved another—a man who in no way compared with
Apollo—but that is often the case. So when Apollo was
away, this man would visit her. The white crow, which
was kept in its cage, would see them meet, but it never
said a word around them. However, when Apollo
returned home, the crow began to speak.

"In spite of all your worth, your good looks, and your grace—in spite of all your careful watching, your wife loves another. I have seen them together." The crow then told Apollo everything that he had seen and heard.

Apollo turned away. He thought his heart would break, he was so unhappy. In his anger, he killed his wife. In his sadness at losing his wife, he then broke his musical instruments and his bow and arrows. Then he turned his attention to the crow:

"Villain! You have caused me this grief!" he said. "Oh, my dear wife, condemned by this fiend. You were innocent, I swear! Oh, men, beware of acting hastily. Believe nothing without proof! Do not act in anger! I will kill myself now because of grief!

"I will repay this crow for his false story. Once, you sang more sweetly than the nightingale; now give up your song. Your feathers that were once white as snow shall turn black as soot. Never again will you speak or make a pleasing sound."

With that, he sprang at the bird, tore out every one of its white feathers, made it black, took away its song and speech, and threw it out the door. And because of this, all crows are black.

"Ladies and gentlemen," said the Manciple, "from this story, I beg you remember one thing: Hold your tongue and keep your friends. No man has ever been harmed for not talking enough. Many men, however, have died for talking too much!" **Thus ends the Manciple's tale.**

The Parson was the last traveler to tell a tale. Unfortunately, his tale was a sermon that lasted for two hours.

Chaucer's Retraction

The author of this book bids farewell: Now, I ask everyone who reads or hears of this book to thank Him from whom all intelligence and honesty comes for anything they liked. If there is anything they disliked, please blame me. I have written to the best of my ability and would have done better if I could. I ask for forgiveness for all the works I have written that deal with sins, such as *Troilus and Criseyde, The House of Fame, The Parliament of Fowls, The Book of the Duchess, The Legend of Good Women*, and those tales in this work that have dealt with sin.

But for my translation of Boethius and for the books about the lives of the saints, their legends, and teachings, I thank Him. I ask now only for the wisdom to know my sins and to lament them and to strive for the salvation of my soul. May the Lord grant me that I may be among those saved on the day of Judgment.

Here ends the book of the tales of Canterbury, compiled by Geoffrey Chaucer.

REVIEWING

YOUR

READING

General Prologue

FINDING THE MAIN IDEA

1. The main purpose of the Prologue is to
   a) introduce the pilgrims   b) describe religion in the Middle Ages   c) describe roads in the Middle Ages d) none of these.

2. The Pilgrims decide to tell stories because
   a) the Monk offers them money   b) it will help to pass the time   c) they are all writers   d) they want to help Chaucer write his book.

REMEMBERING THE DETAILS

3. The Pilgrims are traveling to
   a) London   b) Jerusalem   c) Canterbury   d) none of these.

4. In springtime, Chaucer says that people long to do what?
   a) go to the Tabard Inn   b) tell stories   c) eat too much d) go on pilgrimages.

DRAWING CONCLUSIONS

5. The Friar "knew every tavern in every town and every innkeeper." This shows that he
   a) was a very religious man   b) liked to stay in inns
   c) was very friendly   d) none of these.

THINKING IT OVER

6. Look back at the descriptions in the General Prologue. Are any of the characters Chaucer describes like people you have read about in other books or in the newspaper? If Chaucer were writing today, what other pilgrims might he want to include?

7. Many people think that the most important part of *The Canterbury Tales* is the General Prologue. Why do you think this is true?

The Knight's Tale

FINDING THE MAIN IDEA

1. This story is primarily about
   a) ideal love   b) war   c) ancient Athens   d) two brothers.

USING YOUR REASON

2. Palamon and Arcite are
   a) two young Athenians   b) brothers   c) both in love with
   Emily   d) all of the above.
3. Theseus told Arcite that if he returned to Athens
   a) he could marry Emily   b) he would go back to prison
   c) he would lose his head   d) he could work at the court.
4. Arcite returned to Athens so that he could
   a) be near Emily   b) show everyone how different he
   looked   c) free Palamon   d) steal Theseus's throne.

REMEMBERING DETAILS

5. When Theseus designed the arena, he included
   a) tents for all the knights   b) three temples   c) special
   seats for Emily and Hippolyta   d) a garden.
6. Arcite was the favorite of
   a) Venus b) Mars c) Saturn d) Theseus.

THINKING IT OVER

7. Based on what you know about all the pilgrims, could
   another pilgrim have told this story? If so, who and why? If
   not, why not?

The Man of Law's Tale

FINDING THE MAIN IDEA

1. Constance represents which of the following character
   traits?
   a) intelligence and shyness   b) anger and greed
   c) patience and loyalty   d) jealousy and impatience.

REMEMBERING THE DETAILS

2. The Sultaness did not want her son to marry Constance because
   a) he was abandoning traditional ways b) she didn't like people from Rome   c) her counselors didn't approve of Constance   d) none of these.
3. After she left Syria, Constance finally landed in
   a) Gibraltar   b) England   c) Persia   d) Scotland.

USING YOUR REASON

4. The knight murdered Dame Hermengild because
   a) Constance rejected him   b) he was jealous of the warden   c) he wanted to kill Constance, but made a mistake   d) he wanted the King to like him.
5. Donegild switched letters because
   a) she hated Constance   b) she wanted a granddaughter c) she wanted to tell her son the news   d) she didn't like the warden.

THINKING IT OVER

6. This type of story is known as an allegory. An allegory is a story that teaches the reader something. What do you think that the Man of Law wants his listeners to learn? As you read further, look for more examples of allegories.

The Monk's Tale and The Nun's Priest's Tale

FINDING THE MAIN IDEA

1. Hercules and Ugolino were both brought down by
   a) an archbishop   b) Fortune   c) their own pride d) none of these.
2. The Nun's Priest tale deals with the dangers of
   a) foxes   b) dreams   c) pride   d) overeating.

REMEMBERING DETAILS

3. Chanticleer escaped from the fox when
   a) he flew away   b) the fox stopped to brag
   c) the villagers caught the fox   d) Pertelote squawked and scared the fox.

4. Hercules is killed when his wife dips his shirt in
   a) a lion's blood   b) Augeus's blood   c) a Centaur's blood   d) Cereberus's blood.
5. Chanticleer ruled over
   a) six hens   b) seven hens   c) one hen   d) five hens.

DRAWING CONCLUSIONS

6. The fox asks Chanticleer to
   a) sing for him   b) come to dinner   c) crow   d) lend him money.
7. Chanticleer believes that his dream means
   a) he will be in danger   b) he will meet a strange new animal   c) he will eat too much   d) none of these.

USING YOUR REASON

8. The fox caught Chanticleer by playing on the rooster's
   a) curiosity   b) fear   c) pride   d) anger.

THINKING IT OVER

9. Even though Chaucer doesn't describe the Nun's Priest, why do you think he tells this type of tale? Why is the Monk's Tale not appropriate to his character?

The Wife of Bath's Tale

FINDING THE MAIN IDEA

1. The Wife of Bath says that she is an expert on
   a) good marriages   b) weaving   c) trouble in marriage   d) traveling.

REMEMBERING DETAILS

2. The Wife of Bath has had
   a) three good husbands and two bad   b) two good husbands and three bad   c) no good husbands   d) no bad husbands.
3. Her fifth husband liked to read
   a) poetry   b) a book about bad wives   c) a book about weaving   d) philosophy.
4. The King in the story is
   a) Jenkin   b) Aella   c) Theseus   d) Arthur.

5. The old woman tells the knight that poverty is
   a) like a disease   b) not a bad thing   c) something to be
   ashamed of   d) like a pair of spectacles.

DRAWING CONCLUSIONS
6. The Wife of Bath believes that women want
   a) to have control in marriage   b) to be ruled by their
   husbands   c) to share everything   d) to be flattered.

DESCRIBING THE MOOD
7. The Wife of Bath's Tale is
   a) funny   b) satirical   c) serious   d) none of these.

THINKING IT OVER
8. What does this story tell you about the Wife of Bath? Do
   you know anyone like her? Have you ever read about
   anyone like her in another book? Describe that person
   or character.

The Friar's Tale and
The Summoner's Tale

FINDING THE MAIN IDEA
1. The main point of the Friar's Tale is that
   a) summoners are honest   b) summoners associate with
   demons   c) summoners are dishonest   d) everyone should
   pay his or her fines.
2. The Summoner tells his tale to
   a) amuse the travelers   b) repay the Friar   c) win the
   contest   d) repay the Pardoner.

REMEMBERING THE DETAILS
3. The demon tells the Summoner that he
   a) starts fires   b) steals money   c) torments both the body
   and soul   d) none of these.
4. The Summoner tells the old woman that he will take
   a) her chickens   b) her house   c) her cooking pot
   d) her soul.

DRAWING CONCLUSIONS

5. The demon doesn't take the horses and cart because
a) the driver didn't mean it when he cursed them   b) they belonged to someone else   c) he wanted the Summoner to have them   d) he didn't want them.

6. Thomas is angry with the friar because
a) the friar doesn't practice what he preaches   b) the friar asked for a big meal   c) the friar wanted money   d) the friar complained to the lord of the village.

DESCRIBING THE MOOD

7. Both of these stories can best be described as
a) mysterious   b) serious   c) tragic   d) humorous.

THINKING IT OVER

8. Describe how the Friar and the Summoner use their stories to insult each other. Which story do you think is better at this? Do you think that one man is better than the other? Or are they more alike than different? Use details to back up your ideas.

The Cleric of Oxford's Tale

FINDING THE MAIN IDEA

1. Like the Man of Law's Tale, this story is an allegory. What virtue does Griselda personify?
a) patience   b) beauty   c) wisdom   d) thoughtfulness.

REMEMBERING DETAILS

2. Walter's subjects want him to
a) give up hunting   b) marry   c) travel   d) give up the throne.

3. Walter tells Griselda that if she marries him, she must
a) agree to be ruled by him   b) rule his kingdom when he is gone   c) always disagree with him   d) never see her father again.

4. Walter tests Griselda by
a) taking away her daughter   b) threatening to divorce her c) taking away her son   d) all of these.

5. Griselda tells Walter not to test his new bride because she
a) is not strong enough to survive it   b) would not understand   c) would leave him   d) none of these.

DRAWING CONCLUSIONS
6. The Cleric's Tale is a response to the story told by
a) the Knight   b) the Friar   c) the Nun's Priest
d) the Wife of Bath.

THINKING IT OVER
7. What does the Cleric's song at the end of the tale mean?

The Franklin's Tale

FINDING THE MAIN IDEA
1. Arveragus believes that it is important for Dorigen to
a) keep her promise   b) be faithful to him   c) tell no one
what she has done   d) punish Aurelius.

REMEMBERING THE DETAILS
2. Dorigen is afraid of
a) the black rocks   b) sailing   c) Aurelius   d) magic.
3. Aurelius agrees to pay the magician
a) 500 pounds   b) 100 pounds   c) 5,000 pounds
d) 1,000 pounds.

DRAWING CONCLUSIONS
4. This story is about ideal love as in
a) the Cleric's Tale   b) the Wife of Bath's Tale
c) the Knight's Tale   d) the Man of Law's Tale.

THINKING IT OVER
5. Which of the three men—Arveragus, Aurelius, or the magician—is the most noble? Give reasons to support your answer.

The Pardoner's Tale

FINDING THE MAIN IDEA
1. The Pardoner says that the theme of all his sermons is:
a) Love conquers all   b) Greed is the root of all evil
c) Pride goes before the fall   d) Everyone should be loyal
in times of trouble.

REMEMBERING DETAILS

2. The Pardoner only preaches to make people
   a) give him money   b) confess their sins   c) be happy
   d) none of these.

3. The three men sat in the tavern and heard
   a) a rooster crowing   b) a bell ringing   c) a boy singing
   d) an old man talking.

4. The old man tells the men where to find
   a) Death   b) gold   c) the village   d) an inn.

5. The Pardoner says that the first person to be forgiven
   should be
   a) Chaucer   b) the Friar   c) the Host   d) the Miller.

DESCRIBING THE MOOD

6. The tone of this story is
   a) satiric   b) ironic   c) humorous   d) serious.

THINKING IT OVER

7. What does this story tell you about the Pardoner? Why is it
   a good story for him to tell?

The Canon's Yeoman's Tale

FINDING THE MAIN IDEA

1. The Canon in the story tricks people by appealing to their
   a) sense of justice   b) greed   c) pride   d) none of these.

REMEMBERING THE DETAILS

2. The Yeoman says that his face looks strange because he
   a) works with fire   b) spends to much time in the sun
   c) is allergic to mercury   d) none of these.

3. The fake coal and the hollow stick filled with
   a) gold   b) silver   c) mercury   d) copper.

THINKING IT OVER

4. What do think Chaucer is trying to say about people by
   telling this particular tale? Is it similar to any of the other
   stories?

The Manciple's Tale and Chaucer's Retraction

FINDING THE MAIN IDEA

1. The moral of the Manciple's Tale is
   a) never talk too much   b) do not act in anger   c) only believe what you have seen   d) all of these.

REMEMBERING DETAILS

2. Apollo was
   a) an animal trainer   b) a patient man   c) a musician and archer   d) a trusting husband.

DRAWING CONCLUSIONS

3. The Manciple says that a caged thing will
   a) always want to be free   b) want a nicer cage   c) need a lot of care   d) none of these.

THINKING IT OVER

4. What does the Retraction tell us about *The Canterbury Tales?*